Augustine

❦

*Authority and Leadership in the
Anglican Communion*

STEPHEN PLATTEN

DARTON · LONGMAN + TODD

First published in 1997 by
Darton, Longman and Todd Ltd
1 Spencer Court
140–142 Wandsworth High Street
London SW18 4JJ

© 1997 Stephen Platten

ISBN 0–232–52155–7

A catalogue record for this book is available
from the British Library

Phototypeset in 10½/13½pt Adobe Caslon by Intype London Ltd
Printed and bound in Great Britain by
Redwood Books, Trowbridge, Wiltshire

To Graham James,
who helped introduce me
to the Anglican Communion,
with much gratitude

and to Dominic James, my Godson

Contents

Contents

Introduction

The fourteen-hundredth anniversary of the arrival of St Augustine in Canterbury is a good moment for Anglicans worldwide to take stock of their patterns of leadership and authority. Augustine was sent by Pope Gregory the Great to extend the bounds of the universal Church into the land of the largely heathen Angles. Gregory was, in many ways, the model of a good bishop. It was he who coined the title 'servant of the servants of God' for the bishop of Rome. He was a Benedictine monk and a contemplative, but he responded with energy and imagination to the call to leadership within the wider Church. He was courageous and had a pastoral heart. The extracts from his letters in Bede's *Ecclesiastical History* make this abundantly clear.

Augustine had a less adventurous heart than Gregory. Nevertheless, despite moments of self-doubt, he obeyed the call of his master and set up a community of monks in Canterbury, eventually establishing a diocese and cathedral there. It would be idle to suggest that Augustine in any way (except perhaps symbolically) is the founder of the Anglican way. He was part of the medieval Catholic Church, and his jurisdiction extended only to those places where his relatively brief mission took him. His diplomacy and tact were limited, if we are to believe even the tenor of Bede's report of Augustine's encounter with the Welsh bishops. Nevertheless, Augustine did preside over the beginnings of the English Church, and his great successor, Theodore of Tarsus, established the parish system in England. Following the Synod of Whitby in 664, the

1

Celtic tradition confluenced with the Roman to enrich the patterns of theology and spirituality in the embryonic English Church.

What is perhaps most interesting about these early times is the sense of the universal in the Church. Bede never ceases to make plain his loyalty to Rome and to the focal primacy of the pope, the bishop of Rome. Equally, the Celtic Church, despite its local colour and its independent traditions, remained fiercely loyal to Rome's primacy. Furthermore, missionary journeys in these times went in all directions. As Augustine brought the gospel from Rome, so Columba, Aidan and Cuthbert brought the Gospel message respectively from Ireland and Scotland to Northumbria. Wilfrid travelled to Rome and ministered for a time in Lyons in southern France. Boniface and Willibrord took the gospel to Germany and the Low Countries respectively. In later centuries St Henry and St Erik would go as missionaries from the British Isles to Finland and Sweden. Christianity was a trans-European phenomenon.

In such a situation primacy was essential, and so was universality. Alongside this, local loyalties remained strong and fiercely independent. The tensions that this produced between plurality and unity, the local and the universal, are clearly seen in the writings of Bede. All the ingredients, then, which remain of significance in the contemporary Church, as we approach the second millennium, are there at the time of Augustine. This book unashamedly focuses upon Anglicanism, but it does so with a passionate commitment to the unity of God's Church. As we seek better to understand patterns of authority and leadership in one communion, we do so with the hope of a future where all Christians will become one. Only better self-understandings within each of our individual communions can nurture this. That better self-understanding is enhanced through dialogue with other Christians. Ecumenical dialogue is the source of positive and constructive self-criticism. Nowhere is this more obvious than in the realm of authority. God's One, Holy, Catholic and Apostolic Church is still *in via* and we cannot afford the isolation of different traditions. That can only divert us from our journey. The breadth implied by such ecumenical endeavour is not in itself the end of our task. For the Church is for the world and not only for herself. The manner in which the Christian Church exercises authority ought to take into account its missionary task and the requirement upon Christians to live the Gospel. Christian teaching should inform society on matters of peace, justice and personal moral choices.

In these pages is set out an outline, a background canvas which charts the growth of the Anglican Communion and the development of its patterns of leadership and authority. It does not aim to be exhaustive. It aims instead to offer the background from which we may work further to develop patterns of authority and leadership which all Christian people might accept. Such a development might then allow all to cherish the rich diversity of traditions and cultures seen in Anglicanism and in other Christian Churches, but it will also commit us to that unity in Christ without which the Gospel can never be proclaimed with fullest effect. That unity must begin *within* communions if it is ever to be a reality for the whole of God's Church. This book is a very modest contribution to that endeavour.

There are many I would wish to thank for making this book possible. First of all there is Morag Reeve of Darton, Longman & Todd who conceived the idea. Graham James, bishop of St Germans, remains a very great friend even having volunteered me for writing this book! I am grateful to Martin Seeley and Andrew Deuchar for reading and making constructive comments on the first chapter, and am particularly grateful to Roger Symon for reading the entire manuscript and offering constructive criticism. Jean Mitchison and Fiona Millican at Lambeth Palace worked hard on typing different versions of the first chapter, and Jean Gosling at Norwich has laboured long in typing the rest. Finally, my thanks to Rosslie, Aidan and Gregory for putting up with me writing sometimes at most anti-social hours so that this book should honour the anniversary for which it is written.

Stephen Platten
Norwich, the Feast of the Transfiguration, 1996

᪥ 1 ᪥

The Crisis of Authority

Authority or anarchy?

Between 1814 and 1846 a plaster elephant stood on the site of the Bastille. For much of this time it presented a sorry spectacle. Pilgrims in search of revolutionary inspiration were brought up short at the sight of it, massive and lugubrious, at the south-east end of the square. By 1830, when revolution revisited Paris, the elephant was in an advanced state of decomposition. One tusk had dropped off, and the other was reduced to a powdery stump. Its body was black from rain and soot and its eyes had sunk, beyond all natural resemblance, into the furrows and pockmarks of its large, eroded head.

This was not what Napoleon had intended. Concerned with obliterating the revolutionary memory, he had first thought of siting a grand triumphal arch on the empty space vacated by the demolished fortress.[1]

The revolution of the bourgeoisie annihilated authority and left in its place anarchy. Violence and demonic forces had spun out of control, resulting in continuous revolution. Napoleon, the dictator and demagogue, styled himself as the midwife of a new civil order, re-establishing authority: the government of France, the creation of the *départements*, the rebuilding of a modern and planned capital in Paris – even the origins of the metric system – were all signs of a new and redefined civil order. Napoleon's innovative authority was stamped upon the face of the nation with the weight of an elephant.

Discussion of authority in the present age does well to pay heed to the events of 1789–94 in France, for those events exemplify total rebellion against tradition and a most terrifying demonstration of what such a change in order can imply. In the 1960s, reference was often made to a 'crisis of authority' and a breakdown in public institutions across Europe. The clichés that accompanied these events became common currency. The 1960s were characterised by the existence of a counter-culture, by the determination of people to 'do their own thing' and by the cult of self-fulfilment; nothing was final, all was 'open-ended'; completion was anathema, everything was 'ongoing'. The dramatic events of 1968, particularly in France where the reign of de Gaulle ultimately was brought to its close, made people recognise that such insecurity and uncertainty had more significant and formative antecedents. There had, after all, been an earlier French Revolution which had shaken the confidence of rulers and nations throughout Europe.

Roots of a crisis

The 1960s remain vivid in their colour with their celebration of a new-found freedom, and the assertion of an authority that must speak for itself and prove its own *raison d'être*. Many of these trends were welcomed at the time, but there were reactions to some of the more extreme manifestations of this revolution. The revolution had a long history, for the roots of flower power, situation ethics and the radical questioning of political and ecclesiastical institutions reach down further into the soil of the Enlightenment. But even the 'Enlightenment', as it is popularly understood, would not have been possible except for changes that had already occurred earlier in European history. The Copernican revolution, for example, dethroned the earth from its central place in the universe and challenged the authority of the Church. The Church did not react positively to such challenges; Galileo escaped the stake only by some careful intellectual and political footwork. But these changes began to establish a new and different kind of authority, that of the inductive scientific method. Observation and experiment combined with human reason could advance the cause of human knowledge. Nourished by these trends, the eighteenth century saw perhaps the most influential intellectual shift of modern times. Undoubtedly, the tools which became available as a result of that intellectual ferment have been essential to the growth of modern thought. Almost certainly the corrosive critical acids which have destroyed inherited patterns of authority were manufactured most effectively as a result of eighteenth-century movements of thought.

In the eighteenth century, theology often found itself close to the centre of these revolutionary changes; three examples set the scene in the realms of history, literary criticism and philosophy. Samuel Reimarus, in the mid-eighteenth century, produced the so-called Wolfenbüttel Fragments. These writings sought, within the context of the Christian religion, to separate the historical from the mythical; Reimarus unreservedly rejected miracles and supernatural revelation. The work of Reimarus paved the way for the historical and later the literary critics of the next two centuries. His writings transformed the Christian understanding of the authority of the Scriptures and thus traditional understandings of revelation. There is still no final agreement on the nature of that authority, nor indeed on how it is linked to wider authority questions in the Christian Church.

Alongside historical thought, seminal changes transformed philosophy in the eighteenth century. One example will suffice. David Hume, the Scottish philosopher, in his *Dialogues Concerning Natural Religion*, produced a sceptical critique of religion, rooted in reason understood as reflection upon experience. Hume denied the possibility of a science of metaphysics, and argued that the existence of God cannot be proved by reason. Empirical scientific research also combined with critical trends in historical scholarship and philosophy in helping to undermine traditional patterns of authority. It would be facile to see all of these developments as either anti-religious, anti-Christian or anti-authoritarian. Their cumulative effect was, however, to require a new and different rigour in arguing for the existence of and legitimation of patterns of authority throughout human experience.

These shifts in thought contributed towards and made possible attitudes of radical questioning which allowed for the growth of revolutionary movements within Europe and, indeed, for the relativising effects of the thought of Karl Marx and his followers. Revolution in France compounded the force of these movements which undermined traditional and inherited patterns of authority. The French Revolution also lent weight to the counter-arguments of contemporary critics and notably to those of Edmund Burke. Burke was clear that institutions must be open to reform, but that these same institutions are summarily abolished at our peril. Perpetual revolution in France from 1789 to 1794 provoked his reflections. The existence of an authority that gives shape to a society and which legitimates certain codes of behaviour, then, is essential.[2] Later experience of revolution has reinforced Burke's conclusions.

History or the past?

Intellectual patterns initiated during the eighteenth-century Enlightenment have made possible more recent developments. Contemporary historical study has been referred to, and in the decades following the Second World War the critical possibilities offered by the human sciences have also been used to greater effect. Sociological, psychological and anthropological study have each contributed to the relativisation of traditional sources of authority. This process has especially left its mark in the realms of politics, morality and religious belief.

Critical historical study presents a sharp challenge. It is an obvious and acknowledged fact that in earlier ages authority was derived directly from a reliance upon the past. The mere fact that a custom or tradition was well established seemed sufficient to legitimate it. This effectively reinforced an honouring of individuals, institutions and written sources which boasted a venerable and ancient pedigree. On a popular level, this veneration of the past continues. Europeans are always quick to parody American attitudes to the antique: any building over one hundred years old is apt to be seen by Americans as an archaeological curiosity. Within Britain, and more widely in Western Europe, the industry of nostalgia gallops on apace. Doubtless much of this has to do with a harking after a lost sense of security and stability, but it also relates to the earlier reliance upon the past for the legitimation of authority. In response to this, the Church can be used as a continuing source of inner security by some. It may be seen as the vehicle for eternal values deriving from God; tradition understood as 'the past' continues to legitimate authority.

One of the most cogent critiques of the shift from a dependence on the past to an acceptance of the value of the critical historical method is found within the work of J.H. Plumb.[3] Plumb argues that 'the past' has always been used to legitimate particular approaches to government and politics, to reinforce attitudes to social stratification, to underpin basic theories relating to intellectual endeavour and, perhaps most crucially, to give credence to different approaches to our understanding of human destiny. Such an approach is laudable to a certain degree. As we have seen, Napoleon, in his reconstruction of France, saw the corrosive effects of continuous revolution and sought to restore a new sense of order and authority. Napoleon's view of his own destiny and that of France was influenced by imperial models of the past. The past was in itself the legitimating force behind humanity's varying understandings of its own existence, governance and destiny. Elements of such an understanding remain essential to our understanding. Edmund Burke's defence of institutions was not simply the last-ditch stand of an old order. It was a cry for discernment, intelligence and moderation in applying the new critical and, in some cases, revolutionary insights of the Enlightenment. The past remains a school for a balanced future. The common law approach to jurisprudence relies upon precedents and an appropriate use of past experience. Christian morality has also been keen to honour the significance of established custom and tradition.[4]

None the less, an uncritical obeisance to past ideals and even past heroes can also be a form of idolatry which enslaves humanity and which uses traditional patterns of authority to support the continuance of the *status quo*. Plumb writes:

> For as long as we can discern, the past has loomed ominously about the lives of men, threatening, demanding and hinting at cataclysm. It has contained portents and omens, one god or many. Its dark firmament has glittered with examples, a few benevolent, most doom laden.[5]

Plumb argues, however, not only that an uncritical subservience to the past is inappropriate and dangerous, but that it is no longer a realistic option. If we are to make decisions for the future with informed responsibility, then historical research is essential for a real understanding of our society and its origins. The effects of this process will be profound and sometimes disturbing. Even into the nineteenth century, reference could be made to Job, to Plato or to Homer as if they were still living characters upon the human stage. Their biographies and their personal circumstances were generally immaterial; it was instead the legacy which they handed on which was determinative. Indeed, so central and formative were their ideas that enquiry into their histories could even have a deleterious effect.

> But now in the Western world few are elected to the Pantheon; one or two, a Roosevelt, a Churchill, a Kennedy, reach the colonnade for a year or two, but the modern world is too critical, its knowledge too vast; its communications too rapid for them to enter the portals and be marmorealised.[6]

Politicians are now exceedingly fortunate if their reputation has not already been destroyed even before they assume power. The custodian of the colonnades has no time to prepare them for elevation; the process of relativisation is inevitable. To change the image, once we have been given the opportunity to step backstage and see how the play is produced, we can never return to that age of innocence when the artificial rain seemed real and the wall of the house was as solid as the palace it purported to represent. Such reflections should not suggest an embracing of an uncritical relativism, but authorities must now be able to give reasons for their existence and their shape.

Is everything relative?

Advances in the human sciences have driven us to similar conclusions. Perhaps the most influential of all of the human sciences in relativising patterns of authority has been sociology. Many radical sociological critics were influenced by Marx and his inheritors. The structuring of a society was seen to be directly related to the interests of those who hold the reins of power. A less politicised but equally radical form of this thesis has issued from the more recent writings of sociologists of knowledge; their argument is that our entire perception of the world is contingent upon our own social context and the framework and presuppositions which this provides for us.[7] All claims to truth are ultimately relativised – Protagoras is finally vindicated: 'Man is the measure of all things.'

Many exponents of this approach did not, however, embark upon the road to total relativism. One of the most constructive books on religion of the late 1960s was Peter Berger's *A Rumour of Angels*.[8] Berger begins his argument by using all of the sociological scaffolding of his earlier work. Religious beliefs may or may not lead to a more worthwhile existence and they may or may not be true. There is no external authority, however, which can offer claims to objectivity. It is at this point that Berger developed his argument in an original and imaginative direction. The relativists cannot somehow escape their own conclusions. In a memorable image Berger argued that you cannot push the same bus within which you are travelling; the relativisers are themselves relativised. Life is meaningless in such a nihilistic framework, and there are clearly occasions and events within human experience that transcend such relativities. Berger referred specifically to five 'signals of transcendence', that is, prototypically human gestures which he believes are empirical,[9] and which point beyond the relative and the transient. These five signals are order, play, hope, damnation and humour. Each of these points to a deeper reality, a sense of meaning within our existence, and thus towards a divine creator – they are 'rumours of angels'. Here is one example relating to the principle of order. When a small girl or boy awakens in the night, perhaps from a bad dream, the mother will often come to comfort the child. She will offer words of reassurance: 'Don't be afraid – everything is in order, everything is all right.' In her trust the child will return to sleep. Berger asks:

> Yet this common scene raises a far from ordinary question, which immediately introduces a religious dimension: is the mother lying to the child? The answer, in the most profound sense, can be 'no' only if there is some truth in the religious interpretation of human existence.... Why? Because the reassurance, transcending the immediately present two individuals and their situation, implies a statement about reality as such.[10]

The point of this reference to Berger's book is to demonstrate both the critical and also the constructive elements within a sociological critique of our understanding of traditional structures of knowledge, belief and authority. As with the critical historian, authority can no longer be asserted simply because it is legitimised by the past, by the *status quo* or even because its promulgations decree so *tout court*. Our knowledge of society and its relativities require the application of reason, and the acceptance that institutions and even structures of knowledge may be capable of modification and transformation. The conclusions begin to point beyond simple relativisation towards a more subtle and complex reality.

Individualism or community?

Other contemporary trends have also served to undermine authority structures. One of the all-pervading movements during the 1960s was the 'cult of self-fulfilment'. This trend was in itself derivative of a more fundamental drive towards individualism within Western culture. The impact of psychological theories was very significant here; a parallel influence was that of existentialist philosophy and its beneficiaries. To some degree one accompanied the other. Psychology helped shape, for example, the child-centred approach to education which dominated the second generation post-war period. Educational patterns help set the scene for the next adult generation. Clinical psychologists, and the non-directive counselling methods which became popular in the 1960s, emphasised the need for people to 'become who they are'. Individuals were not to be shackled by the irrational guilt generated by authoritarian moral theories and by an autocratic authority system. Theories of moral development stressed the importance of the move from moral heteronomy to moral autonomy; each individual must appropriate the ability to make decisions based on an internalised set of moral principles.

Popularly, these moves which we have described were easily misconstrued or distorted. Despite the fact that during that same period social psychology received significant boosts in its importance, individualism often still triumphed at the popular level. Instead of pressing for interpersonal fulfilment, the stress easily shifted to the individual. One of the most vivid symbols of this shift in emphasis away from common authority patterns and institutional morals towards individualism was the growth of so-called 'situation ethics'.[11] Moral decision-making could not rely upon established authorities. The action which was right in a particular situation was that which promoted the most love. It was a form of utilitarianism where *love* replaced *happiness* as the central criterion. The growth in such individualistic ethical theory was paralleled in the work of a number of secular moral philosophers.[12] There are no longer universal moral norms and there is no objectivity about our moral experience. Morality is remade in the mind of each individual. The threatened disappearance of objectivity in morals again presented serious questions to previously assumed attitudes to authority. Christian moral teaching, whether it is derived primarily from Scripture or primarily from the natural law tradition, had historically argued for objective norms. Moral principles place a claim on human beings and upon human communities. Such principles protect society from its own worst instincts. It is the claims of such norms that require us to resist the universally tragic possibilities implied by the Holocaust or by ethnic cleansing. Without objective boundaries such tragedies are less easily avoided.

The disappearance of objectivity also reinforces a different but equally significant development, the acceptance of an all-embracing pluralism. Pluralism is a notoriously difficult term to define. At its most general its meaning is self-evident. Variety and difference in the world is undeniable; pluriformity is at the heart of human experience:

> World is crazier and more of it than we think,
> Incorrigibly plural. I peel and portion
> A tangerine and spit the pips and feel
> The drunkenness of things being various.
>
> Louis MacNeice: *Snow*

It is the next move along from this in respect of morality, religion and culture which presents a more potent threat. The rise of Islam has undoubtedly posed a threat to the self-understanding of 'Western liberal democracies'. As Samuel Huntington has noted, for the first time the West faces a non-Western power that has the desire, the will and the resources to shape the world in non-Western ways. The existence of large Islamic and Hindu minorities in Britain has caused people to argue that Britain is a pluralist society. By this is implied a wide range of cultural inheritances, each vying with the next for the validity of its truth claims. Such a theory can then be given a dogmatic gloss. Not only is it true that Britain is a pluralist society (if indeed it is true), but the fabric of government, the structure of our legal system and the assumptions upon which our cultural foundations are built must reflect this. It is, however, far from clear that Britain is a pluralist society in this stronger sense, even omitting a move towards dogmatic pluralism. There is undoubtedly a pluriformity of cultural expression within British society; Western European culture is, however, the product of centuries of Christian humanist formation. This does not require a Christian or Western European imperialism driving out other cultural expressions. Instead, it requires acknowledgement of the roots of that culture as the basis of a Western liberal democratic society.

14

It is the security of acceptance of these common assumptions that allows a liberal democratic society to protect the interests of a variety of different types of minority.[13]

Enlightenment – friend or foe?

It should be clear by now that many of the intellectual and cultural shifts to which we have drawn attention are mutually related. The intellectual climate which allowed such new blooms to flower is that spawned by critical tools fashioned during the eighteenth-century Enlightenment. It has become fashionable in recent years to reject Enlightenment thought and to suggest that we now live in a post-Enlightenment culture, and Christian theologians have on occasions been at the forefront in arguing for this.[14] Although it is almost certainly true that the forces unleashed by the Enlightenment have themselves been transformed by successive cultural changes, it is difficult to see how one can 'step out of one's Enlightenment shoes' altogether and review the scene critically and 'objectively' from the margins. Such a move is vulnerable to the same criticism that Peter Berger applied to his own discipline of sociology. You cannot sit in the bus and push it at the same time. Criticism of the Enlightenment by those formed by it will itself be relativised. This is not to suggest that Enlightenment thought stands above criticism; to suggest this would be to ignore the fact that such methods have a normative character; value judgements are themselves an integral part of the methods forged during the Enlightenment. Without acknowleding this sort of critique, reason, for example, can all too easily be confused with rationalism. Nevertheless, the insights and transformations in thought patterns issuing from the Enlightenment cannot now be somehow dispatched or disparaged as unwelcome 'blips' on an otherwise calm sea of intellectual development. They are now part of, although by no means exhaustive of, a wider history of ideas.

Many of the movements of thought which have been referred to above are arguably transformations of consciousness which the Churches would wish cautiously to celebrate. The advent of critical

15

history has unlocked Western society from an unthinking dependence upon the past. It has offered Western culture the opportunity critically to value its historical institutions, to assess the accumulated inherited intellectual deposits and to understand more discerningly the foundations of authority. Similarly, sociological research makes possible an appreciation of the forces which both prosper and destroy human flourishing. It also makes societies aware of the roots of these institutions and the functions which they perform. The exercise of authority, tending towards the abuse of power, has often allowed institutions and authorities to become dysfunctional rather than helping society to prosper. Reflection upon the contribution of the human sciences is equally important. The growth in our understanding of human nature through the discoveries and insights of psychology and anthropology has been both enriching and enlightening. Freedom from superstitious attitudes to the psyche and the study of personality development have helped people to take responsibility for their own decisions. In doing so, this does not imply that objective moral norms and a common morality disappear or are a danger to human fulfilment. Humanity can only prosper in community, and community can only be built upon the healthy development of individuals who value the interpersonal nature of human relationships. In the past, attitudes to authority have often been too facile. They have ignored the complexity of human existence and the intricate weave represented by reciprocity between the individual and the community, tradition and its development. There is still a depressing tendency to oversimplify and polarise the discussion.

It may be that religious pluralism faces us with our most radical questions. For a millennium, most of Western Europe could assume itself to be a purely Christian culture; there was little exchange or contact with the other great religions, saving perhaps a minority Jewish population. That is no longer the case, and the encounter of Christianity with other mainstream religions, both in Europe and worldwide, has had a decisive effect upon theological method and upon Christianity's own self-perception; there has been a relati-

16

vising of the context. This affects our understanding of authority within and beyond the confines of the Christian Church.

The Churches and authority

We began with an elephant in the Place de la Bastille; the security of European civilisation had been threatened. Christianity enjoys no immunity from such powerful and sometimes corrosive movements. Brief reflection on the historical–critical method and the Bible imply as much. Of course, such theories always retain an element of provisionality. Nevertheless, critical research has affected our understanding of the authority of the Bible just as scientific research has had wide-ranging effects upon our understanding of our world. Insecurities raised by such methods have led to a renewed fundamentalism within certain parts of the Christian Church, fundamentalisms which seek to protect the authority of the Bible in some pristine state, untouched by the acids of the Enlightenment and critical scholarship. Ironically, those who seek to defend such fundamentalisms find themselves relying upon precisely those tools of critical thought which have been fashioned by the Enlightenment.[15] Reversing the metaphor, you cannot sit inside while you are pushing the bus.

More recently, these same tools have been used in relation to doctrinal criticism.[16] Historical research enables scholars better to understand the processes behind the formulation of creeds and other doctrinal statements. The results of doctrinal research are by no means agreed and final, but the scholarly community cannot retreat to an earlier pre-critical phase. But criticism is not synonymous with reductionism; to understand how a particular formulary came to be, and to investigate the ecclesiastical and political pressures which affected its formulation, do not deny the truth value of the statement or creed. Still more controversially, sociological study has allowed scholars to understand better the authority structures of the Christian Church and something of how they have developed. Most recently, this same sociological method has been applied to the documents of the New Testament. Again, this does not automatically undermine the significance or the coherence of these various authorities. Indeed, the reverse may sometimes be the case, since sociology can suggest how authorities, sacred or secular, can be functionally essential to the prospering of an institution. Sociological study is not *per se* anarchic in its conclusions.

Nevertheless, the transformation of authority and the parallel undermining of an automatic legitimation of that same authority in the past raises questions as to the most appropriate forms of leadership and means of legislating in the contemporary Christian Church. Plumb writes:

> Even the Churches, the institutions in which the past plays so dominant and so sacred a role, are paying far less attention to ancient attitudes. The Archbishop of Canterbury embraces the Pope of Rome; Methodists communicate in St Paul's Cathedral. The rack and the anathema are put away. The sanctions of the past for ecclesiastical government and behaviour are losing their efficacy.[17]

The significance of these moves is reinforced by reference to another part of Plumb's argument, where he is emphasising the importance of the past for the growth of early Christianity:

> The changeover from the pagan to Christian ideology was particularly seminal. The delay of the Second Coming, the development of an organised, hierarchical Church, the growth of the concept of heresy, and the final marriage between Church and State created a need in the fourth century to explain a past in a way which differed profoundly from that employed by pagan historians. . . . Again, the definition of heresy relied on decisions of historical synods and councils; the relations between Church and State, which ranged widely over property and privileges, again needed the authenticity of document. And the result had to be so much more exclusive than pagan history.[18]

This quotation indicates that not only the development of the critical method, but also the link between authority, and synods and councils goes back to earliest Christian times. It was the decisions of such councils, combined with the leadership and intellectual authority of specific bishops (namely, Augustine and Gregory the Great) that assisted the Christian Church in the development of its structures of government. We see a distinction between two specific understandings of the term 'authority'. There is reference to instruments of authority and those who find themselves in authority. There is also reference to specific figures being drawn upon as 'an authority' in particular areas of theological endeavour.

Augustine of Hippo is significant in both these areas. During the later fourth and early fifth centuries, Augustine had specific authority in the Church at Hippo and, through his episcopacy, in other councils of the Church if and when they were summoned. In the centuries that have followed Augustine has remained an authority through the influence and importance of his writings. Obviously, examples can be identified where individuals were endowed with authority in only one of these two senses. The vast majority of bishops, for example, in both the early Church and since, were significant at that period only for the authority they exercised within the councils of the Church and in relation to their own jurisdiction. Similarly, other great scholars continue to remain authorities within Christian doctrinal scholarship through their writings only, and not as erstwhile hierarchs of the Church: two obvious examples would be Origen and St Thomas Aquinas. The *Shorter Oxford English Dictionary* reinforces this distinction by distinguishing between two different uses of the word authority, that is, either power to enforce obedience, or power to influence action, opinion or belief. There is a distinction, for example, between the authority of the Bible, of the writings of the Fathers, of the Thirty-Nine Articles and the Book of Common Prayer on the one hand, and of the pope, the archbishop of Canterbury, the College of Bishops and the Lambeth Conference on the other. The two are not unrelated, but require careful analysis in terms of their own function and their relationship to each other.

In reflecting upon different understandings of authority, distinctions between authority and power should not be forgotten. The two words are easily used synonymously, offering the potential for disastrous consequences. On occasions, in the life of the Church, as in human experience more generally, authority has fallen out of favour owing to the abuse of power, and not simply on account of inadequate structures. Numerous examples can be given to illustrate the fact that power may be exerted without authority. Power may be exerted through blackmail or manipulation. It may also be exerted through brute force. A military dictatorship exemplifies this truth most clearly. It is also the case that appropriate and accepted figures/structures of authority may exercise their power in an inappropriate manner. Finally, it is also the case that authority may exist without power. This is true of both documents and individuals. A document may be an authority on a particular subject, but there may be no means or benefit in it exerting power within an institution. Likewise, individual figures within the Church may have authority but relatively little power. The archbishop of Canterbury has an authority through a primacy of honour within the Anglican Communion, but little power to effect changes directly. Indeed, it is argued by some that part of the weakness in the so-called 'dispersed authority structures' of Anglicanism are that they do not realistically allow authority to be exercised in the Church by the bishops and other agencies (synods etc.) to whom in theory we have imputed authority. The limits imposed are too great, and interdependence effectively becomes independence. Authority remains purely notional or theoretical.

Is the crisis over?

How, then, should we assess the claims that generally in society we continue to face a crisis of authority? In an essay delivered in 1988, Robert Runcie, then archbishop of Canterbury, wrote:

> A few years ago it would have seemed realistic to talk about the collapse of authority. Rebellion thrived in the home and on the campus, in church and state. At that time authority was seen as the enemy of personal freedom and of individual

fulfilment. It stood in the way of personal integrity and authenticity, and so far from being necessarily wise and benevolent it was popularly thought to be unintelligent if not inhuman.[19] . . . The truth is that the situation which confronts us in 1988 is very different. Now we must speak, not only of the crisis of authority but also of its comeback.[20]

The archbishop continued by citing examples of a new assertion of authority, from the extreme of fundamentalist Islam to the growth of the New Right with its apparent accompanying moral conservatism. It may be less clear now, not even ten years later, however, whether these forces are as potent as they then seemed, or indeed whether there has been a real swing back to a belief in more traditional forms of authority, rooted in the institutions of Church and State. Much capital has been made of the shift in academic circles to a new conservatism, a new embracing of theistic belief, and a renewed acceptance of patterns of authority. These shifts do seem to be real rather than apparent, but it is not clear that they have been accompanied by a similar shift in the popular consciousness and indeed in patterns of behaviour throughout society.

We have already reflected upon the patterns of behaviour of the 1960s. Student unrest, the Prague Spring and flower power were paralleled in the Church by *Honest to God*, situation ethics and in the return of conservatism in the rebellion of Archbishop Lefebvre. In the Church in this period, without a doubt the most significant ecclesiastical revolution of all was the second Vatican council. During the 1970s and since there has been an implicit assumption that a new conservatism now predominates. 'Death of God theology' is consigned to a historical article in theological dictionaries, and the collegiality of bishops hailed in Vatican II has been replaced by a renewed, and perhaps even increased, centralism. The New Right and the influence in the USA of the moral majority are cited as secular equivalents to these conservative movements in religion.

Can we be so certain, however, that issues of authority have now ceased to be controversial? Is there really a general shift back towards the *status quo*?[21] Other issues continue to test notions of authority

21

in the Church. In November 1992, the General Synod of the Church of England voted by majorities in each house (admittedly narrow in the house of laity) to proceed with legislation to allow women to be ordained to the priesthood. Controversy has continued following the ordination of women both within and beyond the Church of England. Pope John Paul II expressed his objections through an apostolic letter. He had earlier made clear the effects which he saw this would have upon the relationship between the Roman Catholic Church and the Anglican Communion worldwide. Much of this controversy relates to the issue of authority. Does the Church of England, or indeed does even the universal Church of God, have the authority to make such a decision in relation to the priesthood? If the Church does have such authority, how should it be exercised and how should decisions be made? Furthermore, if the Church is still faced with radical questions on authority, what is the situation in wider society?

At the very end of the 1994 feature film *Four Weddings and a Funeral*, the hero, standing in the pouring rain, says these words to the heroine of the story:

> Do you think, after we've dried off, after we've spent lots more time together, you might agree not to marry me? And, do you think not being married to me might be something you could consider doing for the rest of your life? Do you?

Is the final message of the film one which is meant to subvert the traditional institutions of marriage? Or does the film describe a situation which now obtains effectively in British society and which is legitimised by the simple authority of a new *status quo* – cohabitation is a fact of life? Of course, the words quoted are particularly ironic since they assume a lifelong commitment, and that implies something which is not quite so easily distinguished from marriage as a casual or limited period of cohabitation. This vignette suggests that authority remains a curiously elusive concept. It does not describe moral anarchy or the collapse of norms. The issues are complex and presuppose an intricate tapestry woven within contemporary society where sacred and secular are not easily isolated from each other.

Napoleon's reassertion of authority was symbolised in a decaying elephant. The reality, however, was more subtle. Order, and the acceptance that members of a society have a responsibility to each other were of the essence. The Christian Churches, alongside wider society, continue to struggle with this. Roman Catholicism and Orthodoxy reaffirm traditional styles and patterns of authority, sometimes in the face of rebellion.[22] Anglicanism, with its Anglo-Saxon roots, has taken a different path. Its embracing of reason alongside Scripture and tradition and its allowance of conscientious dissent makes it more vulnerable still to challenges to and changes in patterns of authority. What is an appropriate attitude to authority within the Christian Church at the present time? What can Anglican thought and practice contribute to such attitudes and to the development of a clear but nuanced Christian exercise of authority? And what part does the leadership of the archbishop of Canterbury play in such patterns of authority?

⧯ 2 ⧯

By What Authority?

A new teaching or a developing authority?

And as Jesus was walking in the temple, the chief priests and
the scribes and the elders came to him, and they said to him:
'By what authority are you doing these things, or who gave
you this authority to do them?'

(Mark 11:27–28)

Confusion, uncertainty and change in our understanding of
authority dates back well beyond the French Revolution. Our first
chapter hinted as much with its references to Copernicus and to
the effects of Enlightenment thought. The above quotation from the
New Testament makes it clear that the debate about authority
within the Judaeo-Christian tradition has a very long pedigree. If
this encounter with the chief priests, scribes and elders reflects a
negative response to Jesus's authority then elsewhere in the gospel
we discover the opposite. Following Jesus's curing of the man with
an unclean spirit, the crowd responds enthusiastically:

'What is this? A new teaching! With authority he commands
even the unclean spirits, and they obey him.' And at once his
fame spread everywhere, throughout all the surrounding
regions of Galilee.'

(Mark 1:27–28)

Authority is a recurrent theme within the gospels, and should not
be portrayed as an anti-Christian concept. These New Testament

24

quotations highlight two of the main themes relating to authority within the Christian tradition. These are *sources* of authority and *development and change* in our understanding of authority. In our first quotation, the Jewish establishment is keen to know the source of Jesus's authority. Depending upon which rabbinic school one might cite, the law, the prophets and the developing tradition were all possible sources. In Mark's gospel Jesus adopts a radical stance to the Jewish law. It is stated with great directness as he makes clear his attitude to the sabbath:

> And he said to them, 'The sabbath was made for man, not man for the sabbath; so the Son of Man is Lord even of the sabbath.'

(Mark 2:27–28)

References to the Son of Man in the New Testament are notoriously difficult to interpret. In this case, however, the majority of commentators assume that the reference to the Lord of the sabbath is a later redaction, a Christian comment affirming that Jesus is Lord of all that belongs to humanity, including the sabbath.[1] In other words, even if the precise quotation is not from Jesus, the earliest Christian community was claiming him as an essential and perhaps even *the* final source of authority.

This assumption directs us immediately to the second main point, that of development and change in the concept of authority. Presumably the Jewish establishment had already seen a threat to its own position in the teaching of Jesus (or at least this is the force of the argument in Mark's gospel), and surmised that the followers of Jesus saw their leader as the ultimate source of authority. In the first chapter of Mark's gospel, the crowd sees this shift in focus as refreshing and authentic. It is a new teaching, and Jesus's authority extends even over unclean spirits. He is both *an* authority and *in* authority. The understanding of authority has shifted, and this shift relates both to the teaching of Jesus and to the new culture which grows up around his followers. Those followers will be the embryonic group and focus around which the Christian community will grow. As the new community extends beyond the bounds of the

Jewish world into Gentile culture, so that culture will unavoidably claim the new understanding of authority which emerges within the Christian community.

In itself this realisation of development is neither remarkable nor radical. The incarnation marks off Christianity as a religion that is inextricably caught up with the world in which it finds itself. Throughout history the expression of the Christian message has been shaped by the ambient culture. In a memorable aphorism T.S. Eliot wrote: 'Christianity is always adapting itself into something which can be believed.'² Anglicanism exhibits this in its great variety of forms throughout the world. Indeed, even in its origins it was the inheritor of different cultural traditions. The roots of Anglicanism lie in the English Church. That English experience itself can to some degree be traced further back still to the two separate impulses represented by the Celtic and Roman missions of the sixth and seventh centuries. These two missions themselves bear witness to how different cultures shaped the expression of the Christian Gospel, through the life of the Church. These differences affected attitudes to authority, among other things.

The Roman mission initiated by Gregory the Great and led by Augustine of Canterbury understandably placed great emphasis upon the universal authority of the bishops of Rome. This authority was mediated, as the Church grew in England, through the establishment of a diocesan and parish system, particularly during the archiepiscopate of Theodore of Tarsus. The Celtic mission was shaped within very different cultural milieux. Whereas the Roman mission had been established largely in the urban centres of the former Roman Empire, Celtic missionaries had worked in what were often wild rural areas. Furthermore, the network for mission in this case had been through monasteries acting as centres for the surrounding countryside. The Celtic pattern mirrored the environment in which it was set. An emphasis on creation was predictable; nature and the natural world were close at hand and shaped people's lives for good and sometimes for ill. Women occupied a different place in Celtic culture and offered complementarity rather than subservience. These patterns were accompanied by a variety of local observances and the honouring of local saints (the plethora of obscure saints in Cornwall is just one example); the Holy were canonised without reference to procedures in Rome. There was an independence rooted in a more local authority pattern; a different observance for the dating of Easter survived until the Synod of Whitby in 664.

Anglicanism and Englishness

It would be facile to trace the distinctivenesses of Anglicanism to the idiosyncrasies of the Celtic tradition. The Celtic revival is very recent and Anglicanism owes more to the Western Catholic tradition refracted through the lens of the Reformation than it owes to the Celtic past. Even so, the cultural shaping of the early tradition is not dissimilar to the process which developed later within the English Church following the break with Rome. The subtlety and complexity of this process has been traced with refreshing originality in recent 'revisionist' studies of the English Reformation.[3] The acceptance of Catholic practice and papal authority is vividly described; frequently the energy for reformation issued from political rather than religious pressures. Christopher Haigh's 'tag' *English Reformations* shows how the process of reformation in England involved a series of often inconsequential stages over a period of 30 or 40 years. He writes: 'The Reformations were begun, defined, sustained, slowed and revitalized by political events. So the core of a study of English Reformations must be a political story. And that story begins in 1530.'[4]

The interrelation of politics and religion was clear in the reign of Henry VIII. Indeed, the two forces could not be separated throughout the period 1538–60. Reformation was not simply related to the issue of the 'king's great matter', the royal divorce. The wider politics of the time were crucial. Parliament flexed its muscles, and the relations of the king, his advisers and parliament was at the heart of things. In 1529, 'the dominating issue which hung over the first session of the new Parliament was not the divorce of the

King or the reform of the Church; it was the Cardinal: his rule, his future, and the safety of those who stood against him'.[5]

The complexity of the manoeuvring in those years and Henry's preparedness to take clearer control in ecclesiastical matters and of ecclesiastical property inevitably paved the way for a greater involvement of both parliament and the crown in matters of the Church. The seeds of the later settlement were sown and a particular element of the Englishness of the Church of England had been established; one particular strand within the authority structures of the Church of England came into being. The shaping of the English Church would be fundamentally affected by patterns of authority within English society; this would help to shape authority patterns in the Church, as England was transformed into a constitutional monarchy with increasing powers vested in parliament. Both the specifics of the English Church and one of the overriding elements within Anglicanism had been established through the accidents of history. Thereafter Anglican polity and authority would frequently be shaped by the patterns of culture in which it found itself set.

It would be simplistic to suggest that Anglicanism is unique in this aspect or, indeed, that other traditions have not been influenced by their ambient cultures. Orthodoxy has consistently allowed itself to become ethnic or national in character; frequently this led to the complicity exhibited by Orthodox Churches during the existence of the former Soviet bloc. Even Roman Catholicism can hardly be judged to have avoided involvement in 'national' politics. The Papal States finally disappeared only in the nineteenth century, and the Vatican City still remains a sovereign state where the pope is monarch and head of his own international diplomatic service. In some countries (Poland is often cited) the Roman Catholic Church has an extraordinarily powerful influence in the political life of the nation. Authority within the Church is not easily separated from the life of the surrounding culture.

Anglicanism and authority

Having established that patterns of authority in different Churches relate to the cultures in which they are set, and that this affects relationships with the political order, how precisely has this manifested itself in Anglicanism? There is no doubt that both in terms of perception and reality, authority structures within Anglicanism have allowed a certain pragmatism and freedom of expression to thrive. If at no other level, this is clear from the existence of theological and spiritual pluriformity. Superficially, this is obvious from patterns of worship. Anglo-Catholic churches continue regularly to include Benediction of the Blessed Sacrament within their Sunday menu, whereas evangelical Anglicans often opt for non-liturgical services of the word and of praise. In both cases bishops have, on occasion, sought to exercise an authority banning the most extreme usages. Every priest on being licensed within the Church of England is required to affirm allegiance to the diocesan bishop and to use only those services/rites 'authorised or allowed by canon'.

These differences trace their roots to the developing history of the Anglican tradition. The Tractarians in the nineteenth century, under the leadership of John Keble and John Henry Newman, pointed the Church of England back to its patristic inheritance. This inheritance is clear in the 1559 Act of Uniformity which enshrined the 'Elizabethan Settlement'. This endorsed the first four ecumenical Councils of Nicaea (325), Constantinople (381), Ephesus (431) and Chalcedon (451) as the authorities by which heresy would be defined. The precise wording of the Act noted that heresy only included:

> such as heretofore have been determined, ordered or adjudged to be heresy by the authority of the Canonical Scriptures, or by any other General Council wherein the same was declared heresy by the express and plain words of the said Canonical Scriptures, or such as hereafter shall be ordered, judged and determined to be heresy by the High Court of Parliament of this realm, with the assent of the clergy in their Convocation,

any thing in this Act contained to the contrary notwith-
standing.[6]

This quotation also focuses two other sources of authority within
the Church of England, that is, parliament and the clergy in Convocation.

If Tractarians sought to re-establish the authority of the Fathers,
then Calvinists (at the time of the Reformation and ever since) and
other evangelical groups have sought to restore Scripture to what
they believe to be its rightful place. In pressing this point they have
been supported by Article VI of the Thirty-Nine Articles which
states that:

> Holy Scripture containeth all things necessary to salvation so
> that whatsoever is not read therein is not to be required by
> any man, that it should be believed as an article of faith, or
> thought to be necessary or requisite to salvation.

In the mid-nineteenth century Dean Burgon was prepared to say
in defence of classical Anglicanism, issuing from the Thirty-Nine
Articles and the Book of Common Prayer:

> The Bible is none other than the voice of Him that sitteth
> upon the throne. Every book of it, every word of it, every
> syllable of it, every letter of it, is the direct utterance of the
> Most High. The Bible is none other than the Word of God,
> not some part of it more, some part of it less, but all alike
> utterances of Him who sitteth upon the throne, faultless,
> unerring, supreme.[7]

It is difficult to imagine now how even the most conservative and
fundamentalist of Anglican scholars could assert this. Nevertheless,
it is clear that Scripture stands alongside tradition as a foundation
of Anglican authority and self-understanding. A third partner alongside these two within Anglicanism is reliance upon reason. Reason
emerged among English churchmen in the sixteenth and seventeenth centuries as a counterpoise to unthinking use of Scripture
and tradition. So Richard Hooker wrote:

There are but two ways whereby the spirit leadeth men into all truth, the one extraordinary, the other common; the one belonging but unto some few, the other extending itself unto all that are of God; the one that we call by a special divine excellency *Revelation*, the other *Reason*.[8]

Hooker then goes on to expound why the exercise of reason remains an essential tool in the human understanding and interpretation of Scripture. Hooker also shows how reason is essential if we are to discern the solution to a very wide range of problems not explicitly covered in Scripture. In establishing the principle, Hooker laid the foundations not only for the work of later theologians, but also of the empiricist school within English philosophy. Jeremy Taylor makes clear the importance of reason in theology when he writes:

It is a good argument for us to follow such an opinion, because it is made sacred by the authority of councils and ecclesiastical traditions, and sometimes it is the best reason we have in question . . . but there may also be, at other times, a reason greater than it speaks against it, and then the authority must not carry it.

John Locke was to follow a similar pattern of thought in his use of the Bible and in his exposition of a reasonable Christianity. It is there too as the basis of his philosophy in *An Essay Concerning Human Understanding*. One cannot argue from this, however, that there is one clear and agreed Anglican understanding of reason. It would also be facile to contrast Anglicanism with other approaches to Christianity, somehow styling them as 'unreasonable' or 'unthinking'. It is, however, from this early emphasis on reason that we might trace some of the flexibility and 'latitude' which is often either laid at the door of Anglicanism or seen as one of its greatest strengths. As ever it is difficult, of course, to know which came first. Is it that the Church of England's acceptance of reason as one of the three key elements fundamental to a Christian understanding later influenced English philosophy and ecclesiastical polity? Or is it that the underlying propensity for pragmatism within English

31

society has accordingly shaped the development of Anglican thought? Perhaps the answer is a degree of symbiosis.

We have already seen how, spiritually and theologically, Anglicanism has taken on a chameleon-like nature not only within one nation and culture, but also in adjusting to the adversarial pressures of Catholicism and Protestantism within Western Christianity. Since the eighteenth-century Enlightenment and the development of the critical method, the Anglican emphasis on reason has consequently encouraged a development of critical theology within the fields of both biblical and doctrinal studies. Indeed, it is sometimes argued that reason has captured the high ground at the expense of tradition and Scripture. Taken to the extreme, this has resulted in the development of non-realist interpretations of discussion about God.[9] God becomes a useful, even an essential myth to assist in the ordering of daily life. Cynics thus despair of Anglican liberalism: the ultimate destination of such a critical/liberal theology is to discard the need for God. Such tendencies will develop, they argue, when inadequate authority structures exist to provide the appropriate balance for the development of a credible theology within the context of the Church.

Anglicanism and the Western Church

In defence of Anglicanism it is often argued that it is not a confession or a distinctive creed; there is no separate corpus of Anglican doctrine. Anglicanism is instead part of Western Catholicism, part of the Western Church. As such it retains allegiance to the Catholic creeds, to holy Scripture and to historic Christianity as set out in the first four ecumenical councils. Its distinctiveness lies in its polity and in the way the tradition is understood and interpreted. One of the classical formulae for defining the Anglican stance is in the so-called Chicago–Lambeth Quadrilateral. Dating from the end of the nineteenth century, the basic tenets of Anglicanism, set out for the purposes of Christian unity, were stated as:

(1) The Holy Scriptures of the Old and New Testaments 'as con-

taining all things necessary for salvation', and as being the rule
and ultimate standard of faith.

(2) The Apostles' Creed as the Baptismal Symbol: and the Nicene
Creed as the sufficient statement of the Christian Faith.

(3) The two sacraments ordained by Christ Himself – Baptism
and the Supper of the Lord – ministered with unfailing use of
Christ's words of Institution, and the elements ordained by
him.

(4) The Historic Episcopate, locally adapted in the methods of its
administration to the varying needs of the nations and peoples
called of God into the unity of His Church. [This has been
adapted in later revisions.][10]

The Lambeth Quadrilateral is not in itself a source of authority,
but it does set Anglicanism clearly within the context of the wider
Christian tradition.

Those documents which are authoritative in defining the Anglican way are specifically the Thirty-Nine Articles and the Book of
Common Prayer. The Thirty-Nine Articles issue from the dispu-
tatious atmosphere of the Reformation period and are thus now less
easy to interpret than the Book of Common Prayer. The Articles
have often been interpreted polemically from both directions, Protestant and Catholic. There is thus much to be said, in approaching
the Articles, for following the method of the Anglican–Roman
Catholic International Commission (ARCIC) which has sought to
reach behind the controversies of the Reformation to seek the
common faith which remains fundamental to all Christians. Even
so, the Thirty-Nine Articles do affirm the importance of the primacy
of the Scriptures, the tradition of the Church, authority of the
creeds, and the continuity of apostolic succession in the consecration
of bishops. In adverting to the Book of Common Prayer as a
source of authority, Anglicanism picks up the tradition of *lex orandi,
lex credendi*: in other words, doctrine issues from prayer. Here there
are strong resonances with Orthodoxy. The Eastern tradition, for
example, in the work of Gregory of Nyssa, Gregory of Nazianzus
and Basil of Caesarea (the so-called Cappadocian Fathers) expounds

the doctrine of the Holy Trinity and the place of the Holy Spirit within that doctrine using as its starting-point prayer and worship.

The English Reformation produced no confessional 'title deeds' which compare with the Lutheran Augsburg Confession or Book of Concord. Instead, the ethos of the Church of England was defined most obviously through the pattern of worship established by Thomas Cranmer in the 1549 and 1552 prayer books, which were revised and added to in the later prayer books of 1559 and 1662. The means of affirming allegiance to this ethos and tradition was revised in 1968 by the Doctrine Commission with its production of a Declaration of Assent (largely prepared by Bishop Ian Ramsey, then bishop of Durham). With considerable subtlety this document, required to be accepted by all clergy of the Church of England when being licensed by a bishop, brings together parameters which define Anglicanism:

> The Church of England is part of the One, Holy, Catholic and Apostolic Church worshipping the one true God, Father Son and Holy Spirit. She professes the faith uniquely revealed in the Holy Scriptures and set forth in the Catholic creeds, which faith the Church is called upon to proclaim afresh in each generation. Led by the Holy Spirit, she has borne witness to Christian truth in her historic formularies, the Thirty-Nine Articles of Religion, the Book of Common Prayer and the Ordering of Bishops, Priests and Deacons. In the declaration you are about to make will you affirm your loyalty to this inheritance of faith as your inspiration and guidance under God in bringing the grace and truth of Christ to this generation and making Him known to those in your care?

By using this formula and the associated declaration, the individual affirms allegiance to the historic deposit of faith instead of declaring acceptance of a specific set of distinctive confessional statements.

The inheritance of classical Anglicanism

If the Book of Common Prayer and the Thirty-Nine Articles act as an official documentary focus for Anglicanism, then the Anglican ethos was further defined and refined in the sixteenth and seventeenth centuries by Richard Hooker and the Caroline divines. In his *Laws of Ecclesiastical Polity*, Hooker charts a middle course between Roman Catholicism and Calvinist Protestantism. He was the first to make explicit the manner by which the Book of Common Prayer and its liturgical content established and maintained links between theology and the requirements of an embryonic Church and tradition. Hooker's achievement was the completion of an apologetic task on behalf of both the Book of Common Prayer and the practices of the Church of England. He justifies a particular understanding of royal supremacy. Hooker's arguments required within the nation a broad communal participation in the processes by which political decisions are made, and thus brought together Church and State in a rich interplay. Parliament was for Hooker the institution which fulfilled the requirement of communal participation in political decision-making. It was also through such an understanding that the establishment of a lay voice in the government of the Church of England, at first entirely through parliament, was made possible. Included in Hooker's understanding of parliament were the clergy in convocation. Hooker makes this point initially through a rhetorical statement:

> There are which wonder that we should count any *Statute* a law which the high *Court* of *Parliament* in *England* hath established about the matter of *Church regiment*, the *Prince* and *Court* of *Parliament* having as they suppose no lawful means to give order to the *Church* and *Clergy* in these things, than they have to make laws for the *Hierarchies of Angels in Heaven*, that by *Parliament* being a more tempered *Court* can neither by the law of nature, nor of *God* have competent power to define such matters.

Hooker then develops this objection with regard to the place of kings, emperors and princes. He argues from this point that the sovereign alone cannot subject the Church to statute. His response, however, is clear:

> The *Parliament* of *England* together with the *Convocation* annexed thereunto is that whereupon the very essence of all government within this kingdom doth depend. It is even the body of the whole Realm, it consisteth of the King and of all that within the land are subject unto him for they all are there present either in person, or by such as they voluntarily have derived their very personal right unto.[11]

Hence the crown's power within the Church to make statutes becomes directly dependent on the consent of the wider community as given in parliament. Here, then, lie the seeds of the important part of the lay voice within the government of the Church of England through parliament, as it was later developed within the Church Assembly through the Enabling Act of 1919 and the Synodical Government Measure of 1969. The Book of Common Prayer, the teaching of the Caroline fathers, and the lay voice in parliament remain in different ways sources of authority within the Church of England, and to some degree they have influenced Anglicanism as a whole. Nevertheless, they cannot simply be placed alongside each other as three parallel sources of authority any more than one can cite Scripture, tradition and reason as straightforwardly parallel and complementary. There is a subtle interrelationship between these different influences, and this may be one of the contributory features to the seeming elusiveness of authority within Anglicanism.

Wider worlds

The fact that Anglicanism has itself come to be through force of historical circumstances, and has had to adapt pragmatically to changing cultural and political conditions throughout the world, has led to variety and complexity in regard to the operation of authority. Its status as the 'Established Church' is unique within England. The operation of authority in other provinces varies considerably.

The controversy over the ordination of women in Australia indicated a quite different pattern of authority. This relates to the legal constitutional position of the Anglican Church in Australia and its relationship to individual dioceses and in particular the diocese of Sydney. The Episcopal Church in the United States of America manifests yet a different pattern where most decision-making occurs either at the diocesan level or at the three-yearly meetings of the General Convention. Variety in patterns of authority is by no means restricted to Anglicanism nor, indeed, is controversy over how authority is exercised.

If Anglicanism has been criticised for looseness and diffuseness in its authority structures, Roman Catholicism is frequently admonished for overcentralisation. Patterns within the Roman Catholic Church again have developed over the centuries, and the power of the papacy, which was also later rooted in a semi-secular or monarchical structure within the Papal States, has been seminal. The growth of ultramontanism in the mid-nineteenth century during the pontificate of Pius IX was focused in the fierce debate of the first Vatican council. Most would argue that the results of that council were a defeat for the most extreme ultramontanists.[12] Even so, the defining of papal 'infallibility' (whether seen to be the summarising of beliefs already current among the faithful or the promulgation of a new doctrine aimed at defending the Church against the incursions of an increasingly hostile and sceptical age) marked a shift to a more centralised understanding of authority which implied control over local Churches.

The collegial model of authority emerging from the second Vatican council in the early 1960s showed a trend away from this nineteenth-century imperial model. The bishops were seen to share authority with the Holy Father. Authority was still focused finally in the papal office, but the model of the universal primate which emerged from Vatican II saw individual bishops as part of an episcopal college worldwide. The significance of the universal Church and the local Church were both affirmed. It was a reflexive model. The Church could not exist as the 'One, Holy, Catholic and Apostolic Church' without the focus of unity represented in the bishop of Rome. Equally, there was no reality in any model of the Church which ignored dioceses and their bishops as the focuses of unity in the local Church.

On both the local and universal level, the model espoused within Roman Catholicism assumes an understanding of authority which is, in principle. not simply imposed. The concept of the *sensus fidelium* attempts to capture a consciousness of Christian truth which is held in trust within the community and which is focused in the magisterium, that is, in the teaching authority of the bishop. So it is argued that both the teaching on infallibility and on Marian doctrine is not simply imposed by papal decree; instead, papal teaching articulates that which is already there as the mind of the faithful. This does not, however, suggest that the magisterium has no responsibility in defining or indeed in maintaining the Church in the truth. One writer put it thus:

> In the concrete life of the Church, the two criteria of truth, that is, the magisterium and unanimity of faith, constantly interact upon one another. Nevertheless, there is an objective priority in the hierarchical charism given for the purpose of teaching and passing judgement. The magisterium makes sure that the preaching agrees with the common faith, and the common faith accepts the control of the hierarchical preaching.[13]

Whatever controversy may prevail over the reality of such a belief, the model of a continuity of Christian truth which is patient of development over the centuries, and which is held by the faithful and focused in the teaching office of the bishops, is a rich model. It implies an organic pattern where the whole people of God are caught up into a living structure of authority.

A similar living model for authority exists within the Benedictine tradition. Although the monks live in community and the abbot is elected by democratic processes, the life and government of a Benedictine abbey or priory should not be seen as a direct parallel with contemporary secular models of democracy. The abbot is better seen as a benign dictator. He consults with all his brethren, but the final decision will be his. A similar model prevails with the abbess or prioress in Benedictine sisterhoods. The basis of this model is made clear in the sixty-third chapter of the Rule of St Benedict:

> The time of their entering monastic life, their personal merits, and the decision of the Abbot, shall decide the order which they keep in the monastery. Yet the Abbot must not upset the flock entrusted to him, nor should he make any unjust arrangement as though he were free to give orders as he pleases, for he must always bear in mind that he is going to have to render an account of all his decisions and actions.

Later Benedict notes:

> The Abbot ... as he is believed to act in the place of Christ should be called Lord and Abbot, not because he demands these titles, but for the honour and love of Christ. He himself must bear this in mind, and show himself worthy of such honour.

Benedict also makes clear, however, that the role of the abbot is matched by the demand for obedience among all the brothers:

> The first step in humility is prompt obedience. This is fitting for those who hold nothing more dear to them than Christ, whether because they have made profession of holy service or for fear of hell to attain the glory of everlasting life. Immediately when something has been commanded by a superior, it is for them as a divine command which knows no delay in its execution.

Allowing for modern sensitivities about 'fear of hell', the principle remains. Just as one cannot claim *rights* without others accepting *duties*, so effective *authority* requires some notion of *acceptance* or *obedience*. Immediately we are faced with one of the essential subtleties required for any pattern of authority to operate effectively and gladly. In commenting on this part of Benedict's rule, David Parry notes:

Today such decisions inevitably take in a wider span of considerations, having regard to intellectual and psychological needs and future activities. More than ever before does the Abbot need to aim at identification of his own acts of will with those of the divine Master, for his rights to be obeyed as a master and listened to as a teacher stem from his willingly conceded position that he acts on behalf of Christ.[14]

Reflection on Benedictine practice offers essential signposts in the search for a coherent approach to authority within the Church. The aligning of the will individually and corporately with the will of Christ is at the heart. Scripture and tradition are tools which assist us in identifying the direction of that will. The context of liturgy and prayer remind us of the significance of the Book of Common Prayer in setting Anglican patterns. The application of reason within a life of holiness was one of the seminal contributions of the Caroline Fathers. Any pattern of authority that ignores such factors will err in one of two directions. Either the community and individual will fail to accept authority in an appropriate pattern of obedience, or the structures of authority will become autocratic and require blind obedience. The concepts of discernment, consensus and a notion of the *sensus fidelium* become essential as we continue our search.

The Benedictine model suggested here should not, however, be a cover for paternalism, nor for manipulation by those who exercise authority. The essential recognition of the lay voice within the Church and the acceptance of the integrity of each province both lie at the heart of Anglican polity. The Benedictine pattern instead challenges us to understand and practise these models in a manner which demonstrates a true recognition of our interdependence and our acceptance of the beliefs and needs of others within the wider Church. This requires a self-discipline (both corporate and individual), an attitude of listening, and a trust which is as yet only imperfectly manifested both inter-provincially and within separate provinces of the Anglican Communion

ᨌ 3 ᨏ

Power to the People

Human and divine authority

It may be that the authority predicament experienced by
churches, or more specifically by members of churches, is actually the archetypal authority problem of which all other secular
authority problems are just reflections. For the received structures of civil authority are penetrated through and through by
implicit ideas of an absolute authority, of which all other lesser
authority is a delegated fragment. This is particularly true of
Britain, where the fount of civil authority is the Crown, and
where the Crown itself receives authority, as the Coronation
Service makes clear, directly from the hands of the Almighty.[1]

This interesting journalistic reflection by Clifford Longley contains
a certain irony, for it turns on its head the familiar argument that
suggests that the Church is merely a puppet made to dance to the
tunes of changing secular fashions of thought. In other words, it is
not that the Church has simply married the spirit of the age and
hence become a widow. It is rather that secular and religious, relative
and absolute patterns of authority are profoundly interrelated, even
in contemporary liberal societies where the independence of secular
culture is often closely guarded. Indeed, it may be that state is
determined by religion and not vice versa. Longley's argument in
the rest of his article seems to be that, despite these deep and
resonant patterns of interrelationship in authority structures, both
secular and religious, our contemporary experience (and particularly

41

in Britain) is of a shift towards a lonely individualism which in itself undermines any sense of a common set of rights and duties which underpin the stability of Western democracy.

The merits of Longley's argument are not directly germane to this part of our discussion. His underlying assumptions, however, are immediately significant, for he writes earlier of this shift towards an individualistic perspective:

> This is a complete reversal of the moral ideology of feudalism, where only the feudal lord had rights and all his subjects duties. . . . It is not at all clear, either, what reason this [the shift to individualism] leaves for God, if God is seen as a supernatural feudal autocrat, for the idea contradicts the central idea of individual autonomy.[2]

This argument returns us not only to the medieval world of Catholic moral theology. It also returns us to issues of Church and State and of the polity which developed in England following the Henrician Reformation. Longley's argument implies a very profound but also a very subtle relationship between Christianity and the development of Western democracy. The patterns of influence run very deep and do not allow for some of the more facile arguments often used for and against the establishment of the Church. It is not simply that the Church of England either opted for, or was forced into, a particular relationship with the state. The seeds of some sort of relationship lay deep in the soil of medieval society.

Our earlier reflections have demonstrated how Henry VIII and his successive advisers had grasped this point only too clearly. It was not a matter of the king merely finding any path possible towards a divorce. It was also a struggle within sixteenth-century England to arrive at an appropriate model of authority within Church and State that respected the rights of the government of a sovereign nation. Politics, as we have seen, ran side by side with religious conflict. The power of the pope was challenged, though this was not in any sense a novel situation. Any study of the patristic period soon encounters the significance of imperial politics. Constantine's pivotal role in the Council of Nicaea is but one vivid example. In England the point is illustrated with great drama in the story of Anselm's exiles and his struggles with both William Rufus and Henry I, and with the papal authorities under Popes Urban II and Paschal II.[3]

Divine right

The scene for the development of an authority structure in the Church of England, with a distinctive character, was thus set with the Reformation controversies between 1530 and 1558. Already parliament had played its part, although at this stage the role of the monarch was to remain the key to the outcome. Theologically, the claims for the monarch reached their climax with the doctrine of the 'divine right of kings', particularly in the reign of Charles I. This theory had developed in France and is one indicator of the independence of the Gallican Church. In this tradition there were two emphases. The infallible authority of the Church is first of all vested in the pope and the college of bishops jointly. But this in itself led to a denial of the right of the pope to interfere with the temporal rights of sovereign rulers. This consequently led to a reaffirmation of the doctrine of the divine right of kings.

In England this principle had been clearly enunciated in the homily of 1569, *Homily against Wilful Rebellion*. The medieval ritual of anointing reinforced the doctrine and added to its mystique. The doctrine issues in the conviction that, having a divine right to kingship and authority, it is high treason for any subject to rebel against the lawful and divine anointed sovereign. Ironically, it was through the struggle in relation to this, exemplified in Charles I and his archbishop of Canterbury, William Laud, that the role of parliament alongside that of the sovereign would eventually be strengthened. The final crisis for the divine right doctrine came with the accession of James II to the throne. During his short reign from 1685 to 1688, James II eventually alienated all parties from him to such an extent that they were clear that the foundations of religious and political life were jeopardised by his actions. Matters came to a head with his indictment and the trial of Archbishop

Sancroft and six other bishops for their failure to allow the king's Declaration of Indulgence to be read in all churches. The bishops were acquitted and became the focus of unparalleled popular support. The result of the crisis was an invitation to William of Orange to come to England to defend the institutions of the state against the Stuart king. The Glorious Revolution of 1688 transformed attitudes to dissent and eventually heralded the way for a new religious tolerance.

This Revolution also, however, posed new questions for the relations between Church and State. If the monarch was there through a sacramental anointing and thus through divine dispensation, how could it be lawful to depose the king and swear allegiance to he who had supplanted him? It was this crisis of conscience that provoked the so-called 'non-jurors' who refused to take the oath of allegiance to the new king. Numbered among these were 8 bishops, 400 priests and a small number of lay people. Best known among the bishops to be deprived for their stand were the archbishop of Canterbury, William Sancroft, and the bishop of Bath and Wells, Thomas Ken. All were deprived by Act of Parliament and their successors were appointed by a similar process. This policy created an Erastian attitude which retained its dominant influence for more than 50 years. The divine right of kings was effectively replaced by a 'divine right' being asserted by parliament in matters of authority in the Church. These Erastian and Latitudinarian influences would leave their mark, and it was such tendencies that would be challenged by the Tractarians as the Oxford Movement got under way in the 1830s and 1840s.

Undeniably, the denouement of the Glorious Revolution was, then, an increase in the role of parliament in the affairs of the Church. The supremacy of the crown was now clearly linked with parliament. Furthermore, political differences in parliament effectively became institutionalised in the Church, with a split opening up between Latitudinarian Whigs and High Church Tories. The Tories strongly supported the independence of the 'spiritual powers'. Some of the non-juring bishops began to consecrate episcopal successors secretly, and indeed negotiated unsuccessfully for union with the Holy Orthodox Church of the East. During the eighteenth century, the activities of the Jacobites and fears of a Stuart return to power weakened the position of the non-juring party in successive generations, and eventually they were re-absorbed into the Established Church. The divisions left their mark, however, and the High Church Tories continued to exert an influence, notably in the so-called Hackney Phalanx of Catholic churchmen in the late eighteenth century. Through parliament, the lay voice in the Church of England was here to stay, but the manner and mode of Church/State links remained controversial. Was parliament really a focus for the lay voice in exercising its part in the authority structure of the Church, or was this but the thin end of an increasingly sizeable Erastian wedge?

Erastianism or reform?

Simplistically, the Oxford Movement is seen as a reassertion of Catholic principles in the Church of England which resulted in an increase in ritualism and the eventual defection of John Henry Newman, Henry Edward Manning and others to the Roman Catholic Church. Effectively, however, the roots of Tractarianism lay once again in questions of authority. Traditionally, the beginning of the Oxford Movement is traced to Keble's Assize Sermon at the University Church in Oxford in 1833. There are, however, good arguments for seeing the origins of the movement some four years earlier in the controversy over the re-election of Sir Robert Peel as the member of Parliament for the University of Oxford in 1829.[4] Peel had been responsible for easing the Catholic Emancipation Act through parliament in that same year; he had changed his mind on this issue on seeing the expediency of the measure. The fact that this interfered with the relationship of the Church to the State, giving the Roman Catholic Church an increased status, and doing so through an Act of Parliament, alienated Newman, Keble and others from Peel and encouraged them to seek to block his re-election. This they achieved. Their experience with this issue prepared the

45

Tractarians for the next step, which followed in 1833 with John Keble's celebrated Assize Sermon.

The occasion for the outburst this time was the proposal of the government to suppress ten Irish bishoprics. The Church of Ireland comprised only a small minority of the people of Ireland, and the number of bishoprics still surviving in this minority Established Church was undoubtedly a nonsense. None the less, Keble described this action in his sermon as 'National Apostasy'. As he put it, the secular government was about to 'usurp the prerogative of the Church'. It was the principle that was at stake. The apostasy of which he spoke was what he believed to be an indifference to spiritual values which allowed the government to interfere so radically in the affairs of the Church. That the Church of Ireland was drastically in need of reform and that privileges and worldliness were effectively something of a scandal did not push Keble from his course.

Indeed, the fact that this early part of the nineteenth century had undeniably been a period of social and political reform was effectively part of the problem for Keble, Newman and their friends. The prevalent Utilitarian philosophy of Jeremy Bentham and James Mill was anathema to the Tractarian party. Newman wrote during the 1829 Peel controversy:

> I am in principle Anti-Catholic – i.e. I think there is a grand attack in progress from the Utilitarians and Schismatics – and the first step in a long train of events is accidentally the granting these claims. . . . If granted, something fresh will be asked; say the unestablishing of the Irish Protestant Church.[5]

These were, of course, prophetic words. By 1833 the Whigs were in the ascendant and, following Grey's Great Reform Bill of 1832, they remained in reforming mood. The Tory-minded Tractarians had seen the dangers clearly enough. It was again a Whig Latitudinarianism that they opposed, which they believed represented an inappropriate reliance upon the predominant philosophies following the dawn of the 'Age of Reason'. The influence of reason as the basis of arguments for authority within Anglicanism (for so it was now becoming known) not for the first time and certainly not for the last time reared its head. But it did so, more worryingly still for Newman and his confederates, since the high court of parliament was interfering inappropriately in the government of the Church. Far from seeing such intervention as an expression of the lay voice in the authority structures of the Church, such action was seen as Erastianism and not reform.

Seeds of a synod?

If we discovered an initial irony in the relation of patterns of authority in the Church to patterns of authority in surrounding society, we have begun to discover another set of ironies in relation to the lay voice in the Church of England's authority structures. Parliament gained its authority within the Church through tension and conflict between parliament and monarch. As parliament gained an increasing influence in Church affairs through the development of Britain as a constitutional monarchy, so the influence of lay people through parliament increased within the Church. The non-juring bishops may just have seen this as a mixed blessing. Few mourned the departure of James II. For the Tractarians, however, the increased powers of parliament in matters ecclesiastical was not a blessing at all. Increasingly, Catholic members of the Church of England and those with a more radical social agenda saw the Church's established status as a compromise which inhibited pro-phetic ministry and/or interfered with the true episcopal government and ordering of the Church.

Changes to allow a greater degree of space in the relationship of Church and State, and a clearer place for the laity in the government of the Church, arose slowly and without a clearly determined logic. Undoubtedly, one of the key shifts in this direction came with the so-called Enabling Act of 1919 which was piloted through parlia-ment by the then archbishop of Canterbury, Randall Davidson. A further irony occurs here. Davidson would be seen by many as the epitome of an Erastian establishment archbishop. Arguably, he was the last archbishop to enjoy very close consultation with both monarch and prime minister. He was also the last archbishop to play a continuingly key role in the House of Lords. So the irony is that it took an establishment figure *par excellence* to achieve the changes by which that establishment could be exercised with a greater flexibility. In fact, the roots of the Enabling Act were neither a campaign for a greater lay voice in Church of England structures of authority nor a desire for disestablishment. Certainly, there were voices around at the time crying for both of these, and indeed the 'Life and Liberty' movement, whose great prophets were William Temple and Dick Sheppard, was arguing consistently for a greater legislative liberty for the Church. The real impetus for reform, however, had come from two rather different sources. First of all, pressure of parliamentary time was making it increasingly difficult for the Church effectively to get legislation through. A Bill to create three new dioceses, in Sheffield, Chelmsford and St Edmundsbury and Ipswich, had run into just this sort of problem. Second, at the end of the nineteenth century there had arisen increasing pressure to reform the patronage system, so that livings would no longer be treated like items on the property market.

Some response had already been made to these pressures. In 1903, a Representative Church Council had been set up. This was an almost exact precursor to the Church Assembly, with three houses: bishops, clergy and laity. It was consultative, however, and not executive in its function. Its creation thereafter led to the setting up of diocesan conferences and then parochial church councils. It was through the existence of the Representative Church Council that an Archbishop's Commission was established in 1913 to report on the relationship between Church and State. The 1917 Report from this commission laid the foundations for the Enabling Act of 1919 and thus of the Church Assembly. The Act allowed a far more expeditious way for passing Church legislation through the various parliamentary formalities. Through this process, the Church of England had become a 'tempered democracy'. The Church Assembly, with the associated diocesan and ruridecanal conferences and parochial church councils, paved the way for the synodical system that would follow almost exactly 50 years later. A realistic broadening of the lay voice had been effected without removing the part already played by the laity in parliament.

Some would see these changes as almost a direct reflection of the increasing secularity of England as a nation and the weakening influence of the Church. Others would see them as a protection against a progressively more indifferent House of Commons and as the first steps towards the disestablishment of the Church of England. Perhaps a more objective assessment would be to see this shift as an institutionalisation of the lay voice in the Church's authority structures. Whether or not such an institutionalisation should seek to mirror secular patterns of democracy remains an open question, however, and one that we shall need to return to later in this book.

Synods, councils and committees

The path towards wider consultation and a clearer role for the laity and the Church's self-determination of its own affairs was not without hazards in the years that followed. The most notable hazard and blockage on the road appeared in the controversy over the revised Prayer Book in 1927 and 1928. Behind the plans for the Prayer Book lay an attempt to produce a eucharistic rite with a canon that was in line with the historic shape of Western Catholic liturgies. The Prayer Book was placed before the Church Assembly and then, as was required, before both Houses of Parliament. The stage was set for division, since it was also clearly seen as an opportunity to rein in Anglo-Catholics in order that they might use an Anglican rite instead of illicitly reciting the Roman canon.

These very aims roused the fears of Erastians and staunch Pro-testants alike. Even so, with the support of an undeniably establishment-style archbishop, Randall Davidson, the new Prayer Book was passed in all three houses of the Church Assembly. Even in the House of Laity, well over two-thirds of the members voted in favour of it. The forces of conservatism did not triumph in the House of Lords, where the book was debated with informed reason and an appreciation of good liturgical practice. In the House of

Commons, however, both an inherent anti-papist and Protestant prejudice joined with the combined choirs of Erastianism and establishment feeling to defeat the new Prayer Book. Undoubtedly this defeat was partially due to the fact that the book was to replace rather than complement the 1662 Book of Common Prayer. Instincts and impulses fearing a lost heritage buttressed arguments from the Protestant heart of Britain to bring down the Prayer Book. The unholy alliance of Protestants in the Commons (including many non-Anglicans and an Indian Communist Parsee MP) against the new book put stark warnings before those who sought a more reasoned consultative process as the basis for decision-making in the Church of England. Even the elderly archbishop expressed his alarm. He noted in an official response that it is 'a fundamental principle ... [that the Church] ... retain its undeniable right, in loyalty to our Lord and Saviour Jesus Christ, to formulate its Faith in Him and to arrange the expression of that Holy Faith in its forms of worship'.[6]

It was this conviction, in the 1960s and 1970s, that was to drive the Church of England forward towards both synodical government and also the concordat which allowed it a far more substantial say in the appointment of its own bishops. As a principle, synodical government has a long and venerable tradition. The Council of Nicaea, presided over by the Emperor Constantine in 325, was an early Church model of decision by council or synod. Even though it was bishops who gathered there, the presence of the emperor meant that secular government and the lay voice were not entirely absent. In the history of English Christianity, the Synod at Whitby in 664 also reinforces the conciliar tradition. Again bishops were the essential players, but religious played a key part, including the indefatigable Hilda. In this century the second Vatican council similarly revived the conciliar principle, albeit largely in the realm of episcopal decision-making. Within the Anglican Communion itself a number of provinces moved down the road towards synodical government well before the Church of England. Few, then, would deny the significance of synods in the history of the Church, but the composition and *modus operandi* is not universally agreed.

It is, perhaps, the role of the laity in the decision-making process and the constitutional forms of synods which vary most. Interestingly enough, it is one of the ancient Churches of the East that has most clearly paralleled Anglican developments here. The Armenian Apostolic Orthodox Church elects its *catholicos*, the leader who acts as a worldwide focus of unity, by giving the laity a most important and decisive vote in the choice of its leader. Anglicanism is not alone in giving a clear voice to the laity. The advent of the General Synod, the first session of which was opened by the queen in November 1970, marked a substantial departure from earlier practices of the Church of England. Mirroring the three houses of bishops, clergy and laity in the Church Assembly, it took over the legislation of the Church of England. It effectively distanced the Church from the State to some degree, through its dominant role in the Church. Suitably enough, one of the first issues to be debated by the new synod was the report by the Commission on Church and State chaired by Owen Chadwick. One immediate outflow of this was the Worship and Doctrine Measure which allowed the Church final authority in these areas, and thus addressed the questions raised in the 1928 Prayer Book controversy.

The other issue raised by the Chadwick Report, that of the appointment of bishops, took longer to draw to a conclusion. In 1976, however, a concordat was agreed with the then prime minister, James Callaghan, which allowed the Church of England a determinative say in the appointment of its bishops; the Crown Appointments' Commission was established. This includes both archbishops (except where the appointment is to Canterbury or York), members elected by the General Synod and by the see which is vacant, and the archbishops' and prime minister's appointment secretaries in attendance to prepare for and service the meetings. Two names are then nominated by this commission which are then forwarded to the prime minister. One of these is then chosen and the candidate asked if he will allow his name to go forward for nomination by the queen. The prime minister may select either name or reject both. Experience up to this point indicates that no prime minister has rejected both, a step which might easily provoke a constitutional crisis. There is a general satisfaction that this process allows the Church a suitably determinative part in the consultative process which precedes the appointment of bishops.

Synod or parliament?

There is less consensus, however, on the effective working of the General Synod. A number of reservations still exist. These reservations relate to the notion of the 'bishops in synod', effective debate on matters of worship and doctrine, and the appropriateness of a Westminster-style democratic assembly. The term 'bishops in synod' attempts to place the authority of the House of Bishops within the locus of the synod as a whole. In doing this, however, there is no clear definition of precisely in what matters or, indeed, in what manner such authority is to be exercised. This has resulted in some frustration among the bishops about the effective role of their oversight in the Church; in parallel, it has led to an increasing suspicion among both clergy and laity that the bishops tend increasingly to usurp more powers of decision-making to themselves.

Controversy over the effective debating of matters relating to worship and doctrine reach back as far as the synodical sessions which gave shape to the liturgies later brought together in the Alternative Service Book of 1980. Much of the modern eucharistic rite (Rite A) was debated line by line, for example, on the floor of the synod. Can one expect such a process to result in a coherent rite, either theologically or liturgically? More recently, the debate on the place of the Filioque Clause in the Nicene Creed, debated in the General Synod at York in July 1995, was less than satisfactory. Here, once again, complex theological issues are involved. The clause which was added to the Nicene Creed by the Western Catholic Church (which the Church of England has inherited) raises complex questions of the relations of the three persons within the Godhead in Trinitarian theology. In July 1995, the debate was introduced with an exemplary paper summarising the issues and explaining why Orthodoxy has always objected to the Western inclusion of the clause. A two-hour debate, however, which included the dismissal of the issue as trivial and irrelevant by at least two clergy, and which produced bemused and puzzled faces among some laity, hardly did justice to the profundity of the theological questions involved. A discussion of Christian belief on the nature of God, and the inclusion of such belief within eucharistic worship, deserves more subtle treatment and resolution.

Disagreement over the appropriateness of the parliamentary style of synodical decision-making has been voiced almost continuously since the synod was born in 1970. The focus of dissatisfaction is most clearly seen in the familiar instruction when members are called to vote by houses. The command issued is 'Divide' and, as in parliament, division bells are rung. The requirement to divide vividly illustrates the tendency to over-politicise the work of the synod. Those who reject any political content within the decision-making of the church undoubtedly manifest 'naïvety'; all human institutions of any size and complexity will generate political impulses. None the less, the setting of debates within a parliamentary model almost certainly encourages various forms of polarisation, and the formation of 'parties' and unnecessarily exclusive 'interest groups'. This in itself works against consensus and an increasing richness in the fruits of discussion and reflection within the Church. Furthermore, both 'question time' and the presence of the leaders of boards and councils acting in a quasi-ministerial role, with their advisers at hand, further suggest a parliamentary model which is not even parallel to the position in the State, even were it appropriate as a *modus operandi*.

Further criticisms have also been levelled at the General Synod since its inception. One of the most telling relates to its representative nature. The argument is that it is almost entirely middle class in its composition, with a bias in favour of the professional middle classes. Certainly, working-class and aristocratic participation is rare, and certainly the time required mid-week biases the meetings in favour of clergy and professional lay people who are able to take time out from their regular employment. Having listed these criticisms, how should one respond to them in reflecting particularly on

the place of the lay voice in Anglicanism and, indeed, in the government of the Christian Church more widely?

Consensus or conflict?

That there are significant weaknesses in the present synodical system
is almost universally agreed. The establishment of an infrastructure
report and then of the Turnbull Commission[7] (which looked at the
working of the General Synod among other institutions) admitted
as much. None the less, the principle of laity exercising real influence
in the decision-making of the Church is now one of the governing
principles of Anglican polity. The existence of the General Convention of the Episcopal Church of the United States of America and
General Synods in other provinces of the Anglican communion
bears witness to this fact. As a principle it is sound. The entire
people of God take responsibility for the healthy functioning of
Christ's body in the world. Our baptismal and eucharistic unity and
organic life should be manifested in the right ordering of the Church
administratively, financially and in its liturgy and faith. Indeed, it
may be that shortcomings in the operation of synods and councils
issue from a failure to apply the models suggested by a sacramental
and mission-oriented understanding of the Church.

In recent years within the European Union, there has been much
debate over the principle of 'subsidiarity'. That principle implies
that decisions should be made at as local a level as is possible in the
circumstances. It is a principle borrowed from Roman Catholic
theology. It may be that synodical or conciliar decision-making
would be improved by applying an extended version of this principle
which takes account of the Pauline model of the body. If the Church
is the body of Christ then we should take note of how each part of
that body contributes its own appropriate gifts. If synods are confused with the entire body, then corresponding confusions will follow
in the decision-making processes. So, for example, we need to be
more trusting in delegating the detailed and often technical reflection upon certain matters of worship and doctrine to those individual
parts of the body to which we have given responsibility for such

work. Such an approach would be an appropriate application of the principle of subsidiarity. This does not imply that all such matters lie only with the House of Bishops; the delegation should be more sophisticated than that.

If it is important, then, to respect the subsidiarity of the various members of the body, so is it also vital that the Church remembers that for the happy functioning of that body all must come together. Once the appropriate work has been completed by individual parts of the body to which authority has been delegated, then at the next stage such reflections should be the focus of reflection by all. It is often remarked that the Church of England is 'synodically governed and episcopally led'. If there is truth in this aphorism, then episcopal leadership within a synod may be closer to the role of the abbot in Benedict's rule than that of the prime minister or other senior minister in parliament. On such a basis it will not be a case of 'Divide' and rule, or indeed a matter of party politics. Instead, it will be a matter of helping the gathered assembly to focus a consensus which may be articulated through the bishops as they chair their councils or preside over the synod. Benedict writes:

> Whenever anything important has to be done in the monastery the Abbot must assemble the whole community and explain what is under consideration. When he has heard the counsel of the brethren, he should give it consideration and then take what seems to him to be the best course.[8]

Such a reflection may smack of paternalism, and there is no doubt that synods and councils will often vote to focus an emerging consensus. It is also clear that the 'Athenian democracy' of the monastery where every member is gathered is inconceivable for the whole Church; some form of representation is unavoidable. Even so, Benedict's description of the process of discernment is the foundation of one approach within Christian teaching for decision-making and the expression of patterns of authority. It assumes the discipline of listening and responding, to which we alluded at the end of the previous chapter. It assumes the application of theological principles alongside the exercise of human reason.

At the end of the article with which we began this chapter, Clifford Longley wrote:

> The Church of England clutches rather thinly to the hope that reason, or rather Reason, can replace dogma as the ground of authority; but it does so in the presence of a society which has not much time for such eighteenth-century ideals, and which is less and less governed by Reason. The decline of authority, of dogma or of reason, places all ideas on an equal footing in the same market place, and that which is victorious (and therefore 'true') is that which gains most power. The decline of authority is the decline of any spiritual Unifying Idea, a decline which is just as apparent in the nation as it is in the national church.[9]

There is both justice and injustice in Longley's conclusion. A synod based on parliamentary models does court the danger of power politics. But the Church of England is still underpinned by the doctrines (for Longley, dogma) of historic Christianity; it has not forsaken these. Furthermore, Longley's parody of contemporary society would soon consign us to relativism, novelty or despair. The crisis of authority is related to a wider application of human reason, which the councils of the Church can ill afford to ignore. Reason in the eighteenth-century sense should not be exalted to the pantheon alongside revelation and tradition; reason, in the pursuit of a consensus derived from Christian truth, should stand at the heart of any patterns and structures of authority within the Church.

◖ 4 ◗

A Commonwealth of Churches

An imperial Church?

The scene is an enormous and colourful marquee in the village of Jobarpar in Bangladesh. The event is a celebration of the Eucharist in the Church of Bangladesh at which Archbishop Robert Runcie is presiding as *primus inter pares* within the Anglican Communion.[1] It is a remarkable gathering. Remembering that Bangladesh comprises effectively the joint delta of the Ganges and the Brahmaputra rivers, travel is an exhausting exercise. Some will have spent 14 or 15 hours making their way by countless ferries to Jobarpar. There can be no doubting that this Eucharist is happening in the Indian sub-continent. Incense is used, but it is carried in earthenware dishes by young women to a rhythmic melody and swaying dance movements. The dress is Bengali in style. The communicants extend their tongues for the host, to reveal the vivid red caused by the constant chewing of betel nuts.

At the end of the Eucharist the archbishop makes the point that this variety and colour is part of the essence of Anglicanism. He notes (and this is often stressed) that, after Roman Catholicism, the Anglican way is more widely spread throughout the world than any other form of Christian expression. One of the reasons for this is fairly easily explained. As Britain colonised and expanded her empire, in the eighteenth and nineteenth centuries, so missionaries took the rites and ceremonies of the Church of England with them.[2] This generally led to an understandable predominance of 'Englishness' in those Churches – even in Cape Town, the first non-English archbishop was not appointed until 1944. It is only in very recent years that the Anglican Church in Australia has been officially established; the 1978 Australian Prayer Book was published still by 'The Church of England in Australia'. The 1662 Book of Common Prayer remained an essential link between Anglicans across the world until the past 20 years, for it was the book which lay at the centre of each individual Anglican church's pattern of worship. The book continues to have a crucial significance for Anglicans, but it does so now as one of the documents which helps to define Anglican polity, rather than as the main text for liturgical worship.

Travelling with the archbishop of Canterbury impresses upon one the English and even colonial roots of so much of Anglicanism worldwide. In St George's Cathedral in Jerusalem, and in the parish churches in Nazareth and Amman, evidence of the British influence and even the period of the Mandate remain there for all to see. In Lahore, Peshawar and Rawalpindi, signs of the British Raj and the Indian Army abound. The cathedrals in Melbourne and Adelaide echo the same strength and self-confidence as may be felt in Victorian gothic churches throughout England. So much of this reflects the cherishing of aspects of English culture in earlier generations. Similar points can be made about Toronto, Harare and so many other very different locations in the former British Empire. There is also a clear sense of the respect in which the office of archbishop of Canterbury continues to be held, albeit now with a far more robust understanding of individual provinces having autonomy. This allows them to be the 'local Church' (local used in a technical ecclesiological sense) in that place and culture.

All this makes it clear that there is an inheritance of an 'imperial Church' which brought many positive strengths, but which provinces and indeed the Church of England itself would now wish to place in its historical context and to disclaim for a communion 'come of age'. Indeed, it is important to realise that one of the determining factors in the authority patterns which have developed within Anglicanism is the variety of historical contexts out of which the various individual churches and provinces grew. Nevertheless, the extra-

58

ordinary spread of Anglicanism makes it clear that the growth of the empire was not the only factor in sowing the seeds for an incipient communion. The existence of an Anglican Church in Japan, in Madagascar and in Brazil indicates that Anglicanism's roots are more complex still. In Madagascar, English missionaries also made their way to the island, alongside the French colonisers. In Brazil, American influence brought Episcopalianism from the United States. Other less dramatic examples, spawning smaller communities, can be cited notably elsewhere in South America, in Korea and in Liberia. The story of the Church in China is a fascinating study in its own right. Undoubtedly, the most dramatic example of a significant Anglican province emerging, not from the empire, but in protest against it is with the Episcopal Church of the United States of America. In some ways it was with the birth of the American Church that the seeds of an incipient communion were sown. The growth of Anglicanism has been haphazard and unplanned. As one commentator has noted, 'The Anglican Communion at a very basic level "just happened".'[3] In giving a brief outline to this 'happening' we shall do best by beginning with the American experience, since it also gives very clear clues to the reasons for the authority patterns which have emerged in Anglicanism over the past two centuries.

America and Episcopalianism

One of the marks of Anglicanism has been its continuation of the threefold ministry of bishop, priest and deacon, and particularly its holding fast to episcopal government rather than some form of congregationalism. The beginnings of an overseas episcopate sprang from the needs of Anglicans (the name had not been coined by then) living in the newly independent United States of America. The story is convoluted and complicated by the politics of the day, both within and beyond the emerging American Church. The independence of mind reflected in the idealists who were the founding fathers of the USA left its mark upon American Anglicanism. In 1782, William White from Philadelphia argued that the Church should be structured from below and not from above, starting from the parish and not from the diocese. In this it mirrored the republicanism of the time. White argued that this approach would allow the *people* a maximum say, and it was the origin of the 'convention' which remains an essential organ within American Anglican polity. The convention would elect the bishops as presiding ministers of the Church. As Britain and the American colonies were still at war, consecration was not possible from that direction, so White argued for a presbyteral pattern of ordination by three priests. Eventually this view, however, was not to prevail.

Two conventions met in Maryland in 1783, one proposing someone for consecration by the bishop of London and the second overruling this. Other conventions met in other states; they were often dominated by laity. It was only in Connecticut where the significance of episcopacy was pressed – Samuel Seabury, the candidate presented by the Connecticut Convention to the archbishop of York, was ill-starred from an American point of view. He had supported the bishops in the 1760s and Britain during the War of Independence. On the other side of the Atlantic his fortunes were hardly higher. For reasons of both ecclesiastical diplomacy and legal rectitude the English bishops sent Seabury home 'unconsecrated'. The upshot of this was that Seabury then decided to approach the Scottish bishops. They agreed to consecrate him at their meeting in November 1784. They required Seabury to affirm that bishops exercised their office 'independent of all lay persons' and to declare that the Anglican Church in Connecticut and the Scottish Episcopal Church were in full communion.

Once the news of this initiative became public a meeting was convened in New York, attended by clergy and laity from seven states. Here a draft constitution of a 'general convention' of state representatives was approved. The principles enunciated by William White were followed, with houses of clergy and laity from the different states being set up within the convention. The convention would keep closely in step with the doctrine and liturgy of the Church of England. The convention adopted the name Protestant Episcopal Church of the United States of America. Seabury set up a rival convention. Eventually the elected 'general convention' came to an agreement with the archbishop of Canterbury, and an Act of Parliament allowed English bishops to consecrate those who were citizens 'outside His Majesty's dominions'. This left matters in some confusion. Seabury was unpopular in the USA for the reasons mentioned earlier and, although there were now bishops in the American Church, the tension between this episcopal authority and the voice of the laity (which they saw as representing their natural rights) remained strong.

The Protestant Episcopal Church did, however, grow and the tension described eventually produced a healthy working relationship within an episcopally ordered Church which took seriously the importance of lay involvement. It is this tension, however, that has led to differing perceptions and moods within American Anglican spheres of influence, and those provinces which more directly derive from the Church of England. These differing perceptions have at times led to tensions within the Anglican Communion since they amount to different approaches to authority in different provinces. These differences have required the communion to request the integrity of each province, and have thus also helped to determine the patterns of 'dispersed authority' and 'provincial autonomy' which have come to characterise authority patterns within the communion. Although the structure of synodical government within the Church of England now largely parallels patterns within the Episcopal Church of the USA, nevertheless the independent 'natural rights' basis of thinking in the founding fathers of the Church continues to lend a distinctive flavour to the ecclesiastical polity within those parts of Anglicanism which fall within its former spheres of influence.

Other early developments

Fairly close by, in Nova Scotia, similar needs for episcopal leadership emerged during this same period. In North America, politically with the establishment of the USA and ecclesiastically with the presence of many Lutherans, Presbyterians, Congregationalists and

Roman Catholics, Anglicanism was perceived as being under threat. It was agreed that a bishop should be appointed, and that with the lieutenant-governor he should be a partner in the civil government of the colony. Charles Inglis, the bishop appointed, was of Irish descent and had been Rector of Holy Trinity, New York. In Nova Scotia he had a tough and unenviable task, due to low morale and lack of both clergy and funds. Relationships with the clergy and the civil government proved difficult, and it was effectively the arch-bishop of Canterbury's support which helped to establish effective episcopal authority in Nova Scotia. In 1773, following the division of Canada into Upper and Lower Canada (Ontario and Quebec) in 1771, the diocese of Quebec was carved out of his diocese. The first bishop of Quebec experienced similar difficulties owing to the same sort of problems faced by Inglis.

In the 1820s, the Society for the Propagation of the Gospel (SPG), which had also been involved in Canada, pressed for a bishopric to be set up in the West Indies. Since this coincided with a desire on the part of the government to ameliorate the condition of the slaves, the prime minister, George Canning, agreed to set up two West Indian dioceses in Barbados and Jamaica. The involve-ment of the government in both Canada and the West Indies, and indeed its financing of colonial bishoprics, shows just how closely empire and Church did relate, even at times on social policy, namely the West Indian slaves. In the 1830s, however, the repeal of the Test and Corporation Acts and a recognition of the rights of dissent led to the cessation of grants for establishing colonial bishoprics.

The development of an Anglican episcopate in the East followed a rather different course. Here British interests had begun with trading rather than colonisation. Humphrey Prideaux, later dean of Norwich, set out proposals for missionary work in the East Indies, but the SPG refused to send missionaries since they believed this to be the task of the East India Company according to its charter. Eventually another society, the SPCK, did agree to support the work of the Danish mission in India. The evangelical revival of the late eighteenth century and the emergence of the Clapham Sect also began to affect mission in India through the foundation of the

Church Missionary Society. The beginnings of an Indian episcopate came with proposals from Charles Buchanan, a disciple of the evangelical, Charles Simeon. He called for bishops in India, South Africa, the West Indies and New South Wales. It was William Wilberforce who followed this up and piloted through parliament a Bill which resulted in the appointment of the first bishop of Calcutta, Thomas Middleton, a High Churchman who had been associated with the SPCK. Middleton had no easy task, but it was a beginning and resulted in the foundation of Bishop's College, Calcutta. This was established to train Indians as preachers, catechists, and schoolmasters. It also aimed to teach English to Hindus and Muslims and to train people to translate the Scriptures, liturgy and moral and religious tracts!

Middleton was succeeded as bishop by Reginald Heber and then by the evangelical vicar of Islington, Daniel Wilson. In 1833 the diocese was divided into three with the new dioceses focused on Bombay and Madras. Throughout this period there were various difficulties in the relations of both the SPG to the CMS, and of the missionary societies to the bishops on questions of authority. Relations with the East India Company and the governor-general were also fraught. A further issue that reared its head was the validity of Lutheran orders, remembering the presence of Scandinavian and German missionaries alongside the English. The Anglican presence in India remained modest as, indeed, did Christian influence in India generally.

When Heber was appointed bishop in 1824, Australia and New Zealand were also added to his diocese. New South Wales had been created as a penal colony in 1788 with a resident chaplain. It was not until 1819 that a new archdeaconry of Australia was established within the diocese of Calcutta. In 1836, a diocese of Australia was created, based on Sydney. New Zealand did not receive missionaries until 1814. In 1840 the New Zealand Church Society was formed in London to promote the establishment of a diocese of New Zealand.

Communion in embryo

By 1840 there were eleven Anglican bishops overseas in addition to those in the USA. The development of overseas dioceses was, as we have seen, much dependent upon the politics locally and in England. It was also affected by the differing theological attitudes represented by the various groups within the Church of England. These differences were accentuated by debates over authority in the 1830s. The repeal of the Test and Corporation Acts and Catholic Emancipation in 1829 marked the beginning of an acknowledgement of greater pluralism in English Christianity. This, combined with moves by the government to nationalise dioceses in Ireland, provoked Keble's Assize Sermon in 1833 and a greater consciousness among the emerging Tractarian party about issues of ecclesiastical authority. Tractarians and traditional High Churchmen were keen to press the Church of England's claim to being part of the One, Holy, Catholic and Apostolic Church, and most particularly in its overseas missionary work. Here Evangelicals and Broad Churchmen took a very different view, continuing to see the state as the protector of the Established Church.

One of the implications of this High Church pursuit of catholicity was that there should be regularised relations between the different overseas dioceses within the Anglican Church. In 1840, a Bill prepared by Archbishop Howley was passed by parliament to permit clergy from the Scottish and American Churches to officiate in England. Communion was thus *formally* established between the Churches. The next significant crisis of catholicity came with the establishment of the joint British/Prussian Jerusalem bishopric. Traditional High Churchmen, Evangelicals and Broad Churchmen all supported this move for different reasons. Newman, largely due to his reaction to the proposed Lutheran participation in the new bishopric, vehemently attacked the proposal as undermining the Church of England's claims to catholicity.

Despite controversy, consolidation of communion gradually occurred. The establishment of the Colonial Bishoprics Fund in 1841 showed a greater sense of responsibility by the bishops for the

Church overseas. Problems with colonial governors did not disappear, and it was often the case that the further the colony was from Britain the easier it was for the bishop to keep peace with both government and missionary societies. Bishop George Selwyn's work in New Zealand is perhaps the classic example of this. Selwyn's episcopal style was not without its problems, but his anti-Erastian High Church approach enabled him to obtain letters patent which gave him rather than the crown the authority, for example, to appoint archdeacons. Selwyn also suggested the establishment of an Anglican province of Australia. In 1847, Bishop Broughton, bishop of Sydney, became the first metropolitan. It was Bishop Broughton who first pressed the case for 'self-government' for the colonial Churches and thus established the path that would lead to separate interdependent provinces. The American Church had established the principle with its General Convention. The call for provincial synods paralleled increasing pressure for the revival of the Convocations of Canterbury and York in England. This was not finally achieved until 1855 in Canterbury and 1861 in York.

Although the British government failed to grant self-government to overseas dioceses and provinces in the 1850s, nevertheless steps toward the establishment of a communion were being taken. Synods were formed in Toronto and Nova Scotia, and in Melbourne in 1855 a Bill was passed allowing the diocese to become a province. In Adelaide, Sydney and New Zealand similar sorts of developments proceeded. Indeed, it was Selwyn's work in New Zealand that was to set the pattern that would eventually lead to the later Anglican pattern of a federation of interdependent provinces.

It would paint an unbalanced picture to leave this part of the historical narrative without reference to those parts of the Anglican Communion whose roots lie well outside the boundaries of the former British Empire. One startling example is the Anglican Church in Japan. It was in early 1859, while Japan was still closed to other nations, that foreign missionaries entered Japan at Nagasaki. They lived there quietly, learning and studying and being open to other people. They had been sent there by the Episcopal Church in the USA. One of these clergymen eventually became bishop of

China and Japan, bishop of Edo, and effectively founding father of the Anglican Church in Japan (Nippon Sei Ko Kai – NSKK). The first Japanese bishop was consecrated in 1923, when the diocese of Tokyo was formed as a self-supporting diocese. This was followed immediately by a bishop being appointed for the new diocese of Osaka. The Episcopal Church in the Philippines was also founded by the Episcopal Church of the USA, as indeed was the Episcopal Church of Brazil (Igreja Episcopal Anglicana do Brasil). The Church in Brazil began with two expatriate chaplaincies established in 1810. Further missionary work, following the separation of Church and State in 1889, was carried out in the southern states, the missionaries coming from the USA. The origins of Anglicanism are very diverse.

Emerging instruments of communion

The rapidity of the expansion of the Anglican Church overseas is reflected in the fact that by 1865, alongside 37 bishoprics in the American Church, there were now 47 bishoprics within British colonies across the world. Effectively, the pattern had become a bishopric in each colony in the same way that the Church in the USA had established a bishopric in each state. The danger of overlapping jurisdictions already existed as both the Church of England and the Episcopal Church in the USA 'expanded' overseas. As we have noted, this expansion was accompanied by a general desire and (since the Churches were not Established or supported by the State) need for the Churches to be self-governing and self-supporting. This was mirrored in the growing tendency of overseas Churches to elect and consecrate their own bishops. The presence of a number of overseas bishops at the one hundred and fiftieth anniversary celebrations of the SPG in 1851 heightened the awareness of members of the Church of England to the existence of an Anglican Church abroad.

The need to affirm apostolicity led moderate High Churchmen to press for a clearer notion of the catholicity of the Church of England. In the colonies it led bishops to claim their seats as members of the upper house of the newly revived Convocation of Canterbury. It was during the 1850s that the term 'Anglican Communion' began to be used of the worldwide Anglican Church. In 1860 Bishop Gray of Cape Town called for an Anglican synod. Gray was a clear-headed man with a sharp sense of his role. This sharpness was further focused in the controversy which blew up around John William Colenso, the Bishop of Natal. Colenso had published two books on biblical criticism, both of which proved to be doctrinally offensive. Colenso refused to be tried by the English bishops or the archbishop of Canterbury, and Bishop Gray eventually took action himself and deposed him. It was due partly to Gray's handling of the Colenso affair that the need for regular consultation between Anglican bishops became clear. There were various reasons for calling together the bishops. These included isolation, response to intellectual challenge to the Christian faith, fears for doctrinal and liturgical continuity and then also general issues of authority within and between provinces.

Archbishop Longley responded to these pressures with wisdom and with statesmanship. The Colenso affair had made the issue of consultation between Anglican dioceses across the world more pressing. The bishops and clergy of the Canadian Church called upon the archbishop of Canterbury to convene a synod of all Anglican bishops, but not including those from Scotland and the USA. In the Convocation of Canterbury, Broad Churchmen were strongly critical of the proposal for such a synod. In February 1867 the proposal for a synod was, however, considered. Samuel Wilberforce formally proposed a motion for an inter-Anglican synod. Archbishop Longley and Bishop Tait of London supported the proposal, and an invitation was sent to *all* Anglican bishops to attend a meeting to 'pray and deliberate together'. With only 24 exceptions (and often for extenuating circumstances) the initial response was favourable. It was to be a conference, not a synod or a council. This was to avoid any theological difficulties that might be raised by calling it a council, in the patristic sense of that word.

In September 1867, 76 bishops gathered for a week of meetings, and the first resolution sets out clearly how the Lambeth fathers saw the function and significance of their meeting:

> That it appears to us expedient, for the purpose of maintaining brotherly intercommunion, that all cases of establishment of new sees, and appointment of new bishops, be notified to all archbishops and metropolitans, and all presiding bishops of the Anglican Communion.[4]

Retrospectively, the shadow of the Colenso affair leaves its mark in this resolution. *In prospect*, the existence of 'the Anglican Communion' is now firmly set in its place. The terms of reference of the conference were clearly set by Longley. It was not to speak on behalf of the whole Church or even on behalf of the bishops in communion with the see of Canterbury. It was a private meeting of bishops, free from government links, and it was consultative in nature.

Longley handled the bishops with great skill, and in doing so set the scene for Lambeth Conferences thereafter. One commentator notes: 'Archbishop Longley who gave the matter [the calling of a conference] careful and judicious thought was well aware that it was, in his words, "entirely without precedent".'[5] In that particular sense, the 1867 Lambeth Conference could be identified as the formal beginning of the Anglican Communion as we now know it. Reports were commissioned by the bishops which were brought back to an adjourned final session of the conference in the December of that same year. The most significant report was that on synodical government and the election of bishops. Also published at the end of these deliberations was an encyclical which, though warning against 'papal pretensions and mariolatry',[6] still received acclaim from Henry Edward Manning, now Cardinal Archbishop of Westminster, formerly an Anglican and generally seen as one of the leaders of the 'ultramontane' party within Roman Catholicism at the time.

The conference, then, established a pattern of authority within Anglicanism. It did not legislate for the Church, but made recommendations that should be considered by different dioceses and provinces. Longley established the archbishop of Canterbury's role as *primus inter pares* and as such gave the see of Canterbury a high profile in helping to identify unity and communion within Anglicanism. The report confirmed the Anglican pattern of synodical government, which in the case of the mother church was not to come into full effect for more than one hundred years after the conference. It also confirmed the principle of self-government of provinces which had already begun to emerge. It thus pre-figures talk of 'autonomy of provinces' which has been so central to discussions of communion within Anglicanism in recent years. This trend towards autonomy was confirmed in the Colonial Clergy Act of 1874 which released metropolitans from the duty of obedience to another metropolitan who had consecrated them, and thus gave them effective independence from Canterbury to the metropolitans of other provinces.

Dispersed authority or reconciled diversity?

The nature of the consultative process at the first Lambeth Conference, and indeed at those which have followed, has not been legislative but advisory. This was made clear at the end of the first conference. As corresponding secretary, at the adjourned December session of the 1867 conference, Bishop Selwyn of New Zealand argued that within the communion there should be no servile authority but instead a 'happy combination of elastic freedom with efficient control'.[7] In 1876 Archibald Campbell Tait, who had succeeded Longley as archbishop of Canterbury, wrote to all Anglican bishops to enquire as to whether they wanted a second conference. The response was positive, and a second conference was called for 1878. This conference established four principles which again relate to authority within the communion. The principles were: respect for the actions of a self-governing province, consultation between provinces before ministers may officiate in another province, the sending of letters testimonial between bishops before a minister officiates in a different province, and the principle that no missionary bishop be consecrated in a place where a bishop had already been sent by another Church of the communion. The intention to avoid overlapping jurisdictions was thus established.

The success of the 1878 conference established the principle that more would follow, and Archbishop Benson duly called a third conference in 1888. Undoubtedly, in regard to both authority and ecclesiology, the most critical development on this occasion was the adoption of the Chicago (and what later became known as the Lambeth or Chicago–Lambeth) Quadrilateral, as mentioned in our second chapter. The four principles enshrined in this statement attempt to define the marks of a united Church, and they have served to act as markers in ecumenical theological dialogue in the contemporary Church. They were set out classically in Resolution II of the 1888 conference.

Pre-empting the thirteenth centenary in 1897 of Augustine's arrival in Canterbury, Archbishop Benson had issued invitations for the conference in the previous year. Following Benson's death, it fell to Frederick Temple to chair the 1897 conference. Benson had included on the agenda consideration of a 'central consultative body' for the communion. Despite American opposition this remained on the agenda, although suggestions that the archbishop of Canterbury might assume the title patriarch were dropped. A Central Consultative Council was approved and was set up by Temple. The 1908 conference reconstituted this council with a representative from each province, two from Canterbury and four from the American Church. The 1920 conference (delayed due to the Great War) reaffirmed the Chicago–Lambeth Quadrilateral and emphasised episcopacy as essential for the Church. Non-episcopal Churches were encouraged to take episcopacy into their system, and work started on the process which eventually led (after the Second World War) to the establishment of the 'United Churches' of the Indian subcontinent.

On matters of authority and communion it was the archiepiscopate of Geoffrey Fisher of 1945–61 that was to be most influential in bringing together the communion as it now exists. With the advent of air travel, Fisher took the opportunity to visit widely in the communion. He was an able administrator and a wise drafter of constitutions. Fisher encouraged the formation of autonomous provinces and was particularly instrumental in setting up a number of African provinces. He also established the model within the Anglican Communion of the archbishop of Canterbury as the final court of appeal. Also during Fisher's time, at the 1958 Lambeth Conference, it was acknowledged that the Consultative Council had been ineffective in its work and particularly in its consultations over the formation of the united Church of South India. The result was a decision to appoint a full-time executive officer for the communion. Stephen Bayne, bishop of Olympia in the USA, was appointed to the post with the responsibility of travelling and keeping in touch with all the provinces of the communion. It was Fisher's work, both between and within the Lambeth Conferences, that helped to consolidate the archbishop of Canterbury's role within the Anglican Communion. The office of the archbishop of Canterbury had itself become established as an 'instrument of communion'.

In more recent years other organs have been set up to act as instruments of communion. These include the Anglican Consultative Council (ACC) established by the Lambeth Conference of 1968, and then the Primates' Meeting which began to assume a particular significance after the 1978 Lambeth Conference. The ACC brings together bishops, clergy and laity from throughout the communion once every three years. Its role is to take forward the work of the communion between Lambeth Conferences, and it superseded the earlier Consultative Council/Body. It is the only inter-Anglican body with a constitution. Its president is the archbishop of Canterbury and its chair, who is elected, may be a bishop, a minister (priest/deacon) or a layperson. Again, the ACC is a consultative body and has no legislative powers.

The Primates' Meeting is similarly consultative, and it too is responsible for taking forward the work of the communion between Lambeth Conferences, and of responding to emergencies as necessary. The joint session of the Primates' Meeting and the Standing Committee of the Anglican Consultative Council in Cyprus in 1989, responding to Resolution 18 of the 1988 Lambeth Conference, looked at ways of enhancing the role of the Primates' Meetings. The proposals spoke of: 'offering guidance on doctrinal, moral and pastoral matters – all matters specifically related to the episcopal office. To those concerns must be added the apostolic responsibility of leadership in the mission of the Church.'[8]

Later joint meetings in Northern Ireland in 1991 and Cape Town in 1993 did not follow up these proposals. This failure to act upon proposals is not isolated to this example, and suggests the need for clearer structures and more effective support at the heart of the communion. It is not a matter of setting up more bodies but rather strengthening and clarifying the functions of those that already exist.

The proliferation of consultative bodies has undoubtedly done much to enhance communication within the Anglican Communion. It has not necessarily increased the clarity of patterns of authority. The parallel consultative bodies have led to the growth of suspicions. Laity and clergy easily suspect the primates of arrogating more power to themselves. Bishops fear that the ACC is just one more 'talking shop', a discussion group with no teeth to make decisions or implement changes. These criticisms are undoubtedly to be taken seriously. 'Dispersed authority' is a term often used positively of Anglicanism in the same way that 'reconciled diversity' is sometimes used similarly in ecumenical discussion. It is always a danger that 'dispersed authority' will disintegrate into legislative anarchy, while 'reconciled diversity' becomes libertarianism.

Earlier, I noted Bill Jacob's aphorism that the Anglican Communion at a very basic level 'just happened'. Part of what this book aims to discover is whether it is true that 'at a very basic level *Anglican patterns of authority also just happened*'. If that is the case, are these patterns of authority so diverse, dispersed and consultative that the communion is purely a loose association of Churches which have a partially common historical heritage? Does autonomy mean ultimately that even interdependence is forsaken? The historical background argues against such an anarchic view, but contemporary experience of impaired communion suggests that these patterns of authority require a major overhaul if they are to be effective in acting as the foundations of a healthy living organism.

⤌ 5 ⤍

Local and Universal

Diversity and locality

Patriarch Alexis II, head of the Russian Orthodox Church, who two weeks ago ordered his priests to stop praying 'temporarily' for the Ecumenical Patriarch Bartholomeos of Constantinople, continues to fulminate against Bartholomeos' decision to take under his jurisdiction the Estonian Apostolic Orthodox Church. At a press conference on Remembrance Sunday (25 February) Alexis referred to the Ecumenical Patriarch as a 'schismatic'. If this is his opinion it is difficult to see how the Russian Orthodox Church can stay in the worldwide family of Orthodox Churches.[1]

This journalist's report on problems with the Church in Estonia takes us to the heart of the discussion about the local and universal in regard to jurisdiction within the Church. In the inter-war years the Estonians looked to the ecumenical patriarch as *primus inter pares*. Since then, and particularly during the period when Estonia formed part of the Soviet Union, the patriarch of Moscow had jurisdiction within the Estonian Orthodox Church. Indeed, the first episcopal appointment of Alexis II, the present patriarch of Moscow, was as bishop in Estonia. It is easy to understand how, following the collapse of the Soviet Union and with the rise of nationalism, Estonian Orthodoxy may be more wary of continuing to accept Russian jurisdiction. It is also understandable that the Russian patri-

73

archate is alarmed at such moves. With the present divisions in the far larger Orthodox Church in the Ukraine, Estonia could easily set an unhappy precedent for the Russians. Hence another journalist writes of the situation:

> Why did Moscow react so strongly? Perhaps because the Orthodox faithful in Ukraine might follow the example of Estonians who do not wish to be ruled from Moscow. There are 7000 Orthodox parishes in Ukraine, and persistent demands for a Ukrainian Orthodox Church independent of Moscow. To Moscow's displeasure, Constantinople has accepted the hitherto unrecognised Ukrainian Orthodox hierarchs in the diaspora.[2]

Both the strengths and the weaknesses of the Orthodox approach to the significance of the local Church can be discovered here. The strength lies in recognising cultural difference and nationhood. Orthodoxy often assists in identifying nationality. To be Romanian is to be Romanian Orthodox and to be Russian is to be Russian Orthodox. Similar parallels can be drawn in Georgia, Bulgaria and Serbia. The negative is the obverse of this same coin: national identity can easily lapse into an uncritical nationalism. Sometimes Orthodoxy can appear to encourage a frightening xenophobia. But Orthodox emphasis on the significance of the local Church runs far deeper than matters of nationality and politics, for it issues from theological roots, as we shall see later in this chapter.

There are clear parallels between Anglicanism and Orthodoxy in this area of ecclesiology. In recent years within worldwide Anglicanism there has arisen an interpretation of communion which stresses provincial autonomy. Although, as we shall argue later, autonomy is perhaps too unsubtle a term to interpret the complexity of the interdependence required in sustaining communion within a universal Church, it does indicate the sense in which the wider Church cannot exist without the local Church. Orthodoxy talks not of autonomy but instead of autocephaly. Autocephaly means literally 'having one's own head'. The head to which this refers is the patriarch of the individual or 'local' Orthodox Church. The patriarch is the presiding bishop within the local Church, and thus also the ecclesiastical figurehead nationally. Autocephaly does not ignore or rule out the universality of the Church. The Chalcedonian Orthodox Churches (those Churches who have seen as normative that understanding of Christ's part in the economy of God's salvation agreed at the Council of Chalcedon in 451) see themselves clearly as one family. They retain their unity by showing allegiance to the ecumenical patriarch as their final focus of unity, albeit understanding his ministry as that of a *primus inter pares*.

As with all models of the Church, there remain drawbacks. The classical pattern, implied by Orthodox ecclesiology, where a family of local (often national) Churches live in communion with each other and accord honour through their bishop to the ecumenical patriarch, rarely works out precisely like this in practice. In England, for example, there are bishops of the Russian and Greek (ecumenical patriarchate) jurisdictions exercising a ministry in parallel with each other. Furthermore, the Serbian, Bulgarian, Romanian and Antiochian patriarchates all have parishes within England. Although there is co-operation and consultation between these Churches, the parallel jurisdictions which exist are contrary to the spirit of an episcopally ordered Church. There should be *one* bishop who is the focus of unity for the local Church. A similar criticism can be made of the parallel Anglican (American and English) episcopal jurisdictions in Europe. It is often argued that the great strength of the traditionally centralised model offered by Roman Catholicism, and rooted in the Petrine claims, is that it avoids such illogical parallelism. The existence, however, of the Latin patriarch in Jerusalem alongside the 'uniate' Greek Catholic bishop belies this. Similar examples could be pinpointed in Ukraine, Romania and Armenia. Each of these examples undermines the bishop's role as the single focus of unity in a particular geographical locality. The bishop is the focus of the local Church. Thus, emphasis upon and significance of the local Church does not in itself demand the existence of parallel jurisdictions. Indeed, precisely the opposite is the case if we understand episcopacy aright.

Local and universal – historical development

Reflection upon the local and universal models of the Church ultimately takes us back to New Testament and sub-apostolic times. It is an accepted fact that, in the New Testament, the later orthodoxy of Western Catholicism based on the threefold ministry cannot be clearly traced; the pattern of bishop, priest and deacon, where each order has a focused role of its own, is certainly not clearly discernible with regard to priest and bishop – the two are effectively interchangeable. The deacon's servant role is more easily identified in the New Testament, but even then it is only in the latest books (namely the Pastoral Epistles) that this becomes identifiable. Here the qualities of a good deacon are spelt out, albeit in a rather pedestrian manner: 'Deacons likewise must be serious, not double-tongued, not addicted to much wine, not greedy for gain; they must hold the mystery of the faith with a clear conscience.' (1 Timothy 3:8–9)

In the New Testament bishops (*episkopoi*) and priests or 'elders' (*presbyteroi*) are difficult to distinguish from each other. Both words, *episkopos* and *presbyteros*, have similar connotations of oversight within the local Christian community. In sub-apostolic times a more sophisticated and differentiated understanding of the presbyteral (later priestly) and episcopal roles began to emerge. For example, in the letter of Ignatius of Antioch to the Magnesians, he writes: 'I bid you do everything in godly concord with the bishop presiding in the likeness of God, with the presbyters in the likeness of the council of the apostles, while the deacons who are so dear to me have been entrusted with the ministry of Christ.' (6.1)

By now the bishops are beginning to assume a more obviously focal role within the Church. Later, the bishop becomes 'classically' the celebrant of the Eucharist in the local Church. He assumes a wider ministry of oversight. On this model, it is the bishop's Eucharist over which the priest presides, albeit that both priest and bishop are ultimately participating in the ministry of Christ. This development, however, illustrates well the growth of the Church, which demanded that each congregation had its own priest. The priest and congregation then see the bishop as the wider focus of unity and link with the universal Church. Such a theology resisted any drift towards congregationalism.

It would seem, then, that the threefold ministry arose through the interplay of theological determinants and a response to local need. In general, early Christianity was an urban phenomenon. Bishops thus had their principal churches in cities and these churches would in due course begin to take on the more impressive form which came to be known as cathedrals. From early times it was accepted that the bishop represented his community (the local Church) to the universal, and was thus the link with the wider Church. The reverse was also true, and the bishop represented the universal society to the local and to the particular. It was generally the monks and ascetics who took themselves out into the desert or the less populated countryside. It was this pattern that developed following Gregory's sending of Augustine to Canterbury. Although Augustine was himself a monk, he brought with him the polity of urban 'Roman' Christianity. This was the same pattern as that discovered by Wilfrid and Benedict Biscop in their pilgrimages through France and to Rome itself. It is the same pattern, too, that St Felix would have brought with him when he travelled from Burgundy to set up the East Anglian see in about 630 in Dunwich or, more likely still, in Felixstowe.

It would be a mistake, however, to assume total uniformity in the historical development of the Christian Church and in the growth of its polity. Local and universal related to each other very differently in the Celtic and Roman patterns of mission. If Christianity was largely an urban phenomenon in mainland Europe, in Ireland, Scotland, Cornwall, Brittany and Northumbria the experience was quite different. In these places the Roman Empire either did not establish itself or, if it did, then the urban network visible in mainland Europe, and in southern England, hardly existed. In these often wild, untamed rural areas quite different missionary patterns flowered. The Celtic missionary strategy was based on monastic centres often after the style of St Anthony's monasteries in fourth-century Egypt. Monks would not live in 'cenobitic' communities, after the style of later Benedictinism. Instead, they would live in their own huts or hermitages, often grouped around one large church. These monasteries or 'minsters' would see themselves as missionary centres for wide tracts of countryside.[3]

In one sense, then, both the Celtic *and* the Roman missionary strategies saw themselves as having a geographical responsibility. The Roman system established parishes, and in England Theodore of Tarsus, the seventh-century archbishop of Canterbury, was responsible for setting up a network. The Celtic pattern was less rigorous, but still the great monastic centres at Clonmacnoise in Ireland, Iona in Scotland, Lindisfarne in Northumbria and Perranporth in Cornwall took responsibility for mission in a wide area. Sometimes both patterns would develop alongside each other. In East Anglia, St Cedd came from Northumbria and St Fursey from Ireland bringing the Celtic tradition, while St Felix brought the Roman pattern from Burgundy. The great Synod of Whitby in 664 is perhaps best seen as the meeting of contrasting understandings of local and universal jurisdictions within the Church. The Celtic tradition with its different dating of Easter and its distinctive liturgical practices retained an independence which the more universally oriented Roman tradition abhorred. As we have seen, however, some of these differences relate clearly to the local needs. Predominantly urban and rural civilisations were almost certain to spawn different patterns and to respond to contrasting needs.

It is interesting to see how, with the revived interest in Celtic spirituality and theology, commentators easily opt for a stronger emphasis on the local, and on the distinctiveness of different traditions. This they see as a Celtic preoccupation. The Roman pattern is easily caricatured as inflexible and unimaginative. It is often forgotten, however, that the Celtic tradition found its way into Britain and Ireland through France and Spain, having originally again been brought by missionaries from Rome. The contemporary debate about the Roman and Celtic patterns of mission suggests a model of symbiosis. Both traditions need each other. A slavish application of the *universal* denies the organic nature of the Church and the fact that the daily life of Christianity is encountered in the

celebration of the Eucharist *locally*. A refusal to take seriously
the universal all too easily encourages both congregationalism and
the growth of idiosyncratic traditions which deny the interdependence of all human groups.

From history to theology

We have begun to see, then, how the growth of ecclesiology was a
historical development in the early Church. We have seen too that
consistency took time to emerge. There is no uniform order or
structure, for example, within the New Testament Church. Even by
the time of the Acts of the Apostles there is no uniformity. The
twelve are no longer referred to after the Acts of the Apostles, and,
even within that book (Acts 6:3–6), there is no rationale for the
linking of them with the elders and the 'seven men of good repute,
full of the Spirit and of wisdom'. Apart from 'serving at tables',
what precisely is the role and rank of these seven? No clear and
consistent pattern has emerged at this point. Nevertheless, even
during this early period the mission of the Church and the life of
the Christian community begins to assume some shape, and eventually order and structure. Local Churches are presided over either
by bishops or by presbyters, and there are hints of universality in
pattern as early as 65 onwards, with presbyters who would function
in each town as overseers or bishops (*episkopoi*).[4]

How does one define when a local Christian group becomes a
Church in that place? What might be the criteria? The starting-
point must be the acceptance and proclamation of a common faith
in the ministry, death and resurrection of Jesus Christ as professed in
the historic creeds. This itself is rooted in the word of God and the
teaching and exposition of that within the community. These two
elements then come together in the regular celebration of the sacraments, particularly baptism and the Eucharist, and their shaping of
the lives of the individual members of the community, and indeed
of the community as a whole. The outflow of these different criteria
will be expressed in patterns of formal ministry which help to focus
the *koinonia* or *communion* which lies at the heart of the local

Church. Throughout such a process, the local eucharistic community thus earns the title of Church even as early as in the letters of St Paul. So, in 1 Corinthians 11:18, Paul uses the term *ecclesia* (Church) in a dynamic sense: 'For, in the first place, when you *assemble as a church* . . .' As his argument develops, it becomes clear that this all stands in a eucharistic context, so vv. 20–21 continue: 'When you meet together, it is not the Lord's supper that you eat. First in eating, each one goes ahead with his own meal, and one is hungry and another is drunk.' Paul's critical reflections reveal clearly his understanding of the local Church as the local eucharistic community.[5]

John Zizioulas makes the interesting point that we cannot assume that this usage is connected with the later-developed understanding of the 'catholic Church'. Nevertheless, catholicity is seen to relate directly to the *unity* of the eucharistic community. The 'local' and the 'universal' are thus both implied, and so Zizioulas writes: 'Catholicity, therefore, in this context, does not mean anything else but the *wholeness* and *fulness* and *totality* of the body of Christ' exactly as 'it is portrayed in the eucharistic community' (his italics).[6] The entire force of Zizioulas's argument, therefore, is that local and universal are inseparable in understanding the catholicity of the Church. The two are interdependent. The local Church is catholic by virtue of its eucharistic nature. Thus the antithesis which is often implied (or required by a distorted emphasis on either the local or the universal) is transcended. It is the eucharistic basis of the Church which abhors divisions and disunity at any level. The structured ordering of the Church, and particularly the ministry of the bishop, is the essence of the wider unity of the Church, as we have already begun to see. The bishop's ministry at the heart of both the Eucharist and ordination manifest his ministry of unity. It is for this reason that a bishop's ministry must always be understood within a community and not as the task and role of an isolated individual. The nonsense of wandering independent bishops, *episcopi vagantes*, is thus exposed. This argument also begins to make clear the essential interdependence of the network of Christian eucharistic communities both across time and across cultures. It is for this reason that *communion* and *apostolic succession* assume importance in helping us to understand how the Church is organically related, both throughout the centuries and across different geographical boundaries between varied cultures. Even so, and this will be important for our understanding of authority within Anglicanism, the local Church focused in the bishop is 'the Church'; one cannot construct a separate understanding of the Church that somehow superimposes or interposes a supra-national Church. The eucharistic community defines the Church. Zizioulas goes so far as to say: 'All structures aiming at facilitating the universality of the Church create a *network of communion of Churches, not a new form of Church*' (again, his italics).[7]

It is for this reason that within Orthodoxy, then, the role of the ecumenical patriarch must be understood most subtly. While it has been the case that he has been recognised as having the right to hear appeals from bishops unhappy with the decisions of regional councils or synods, he has still been seen as *primus inter pares*. His jurisdiction does not go outside his own territory, nor is he characterised as infallible. It is from the interpretation of the first of these points that some of the seeds of the controversy which heads this chapter emerge.[8]

Roman Catholic interpretations

This understanding of the local Church and its relation to the universal as being essential to catholicity has also found voice among contemporary Roman Catholic theologians, particularly those engaged in ecumenical dialogue. Jean-Marie Tillard, a member of both the first and second Anglican–Roman Catholic International Commissions, sees the whole Church as being represented in the communion of all the local Churches.[9] The Church is thus understood not purely hierarchically or juridically but instead through the communion of local eucharistic communities, who with their local bishop (himself standing within the college of bishops of the Church universal) manifest the whole Church as the bearer of God's word.

Tillard's setting of the relationship of the local Church to the

81

universal within a theology of communion was pioneered by Yves Congar in his work in preparation for the document *Lumen Gentium* (the Dogmatic Constitution on the Church) at the second Vatican council. This document itself echoes such thought:

> This Church of Christ is really present in all legitimately organised groups of the faithful, which, in so far as they are united to their pastors, are also quite appropriately called Churches in New Testament. For these are in fact, in their own localities, the new people called by God, in the power of the Holy Spirit and as the result of full conviction [see 1 Thessalonians 1:5]. In them the faithful are gathered together through the preaching of the Gospel of Christ, and the mystery of the Lord's Supper is celebrated 'so that, by means of the flesh and blood of the Lord, the whole brotherhood of the Body may be welded together.'[10]

The developed theology of the Church as *communion* or *koinonia*, however, is not precisely the starting-point here in this document from Vatican II. Instead, the 'discussion' and exposition is rooted in the hierarchy. This section on the local Church begins: 'The bishop, invested with the fullness of the sacrament of Orders, is "the steward of the grace of the supreme priesthood",'[11] and the text then later continues: 'Moreover, every legitimate celebration of the Eucharist is regulated by the bishop.'[12] There is thus also a strong juridical element still in the thinking of Vatican II, which has allowed later interpreters to produce a more centralised model of authority than the emphasis of collegiality in the council otherwise appears to imply. The strong emphasis on the Eucharist and the communion which the Eucharist defines is there in the document, but the argument is not extrapolated in the manner which we later encounter in both Tillard's work from a Roman Catholic perspective, and Zizioulas's from an Orthodox point of view. Instead, the universality of the Church appears to come first with the functions of bishops calling the Church into unity and defining the nature of the local Church.

With Tillard, the doctrine of the Church is rooted both in our belief in a Trinitarian God, and also in the gathering together of the faithful in the Eucharist. Communion is thus both the gracious act of God and the expression of that grace through the communion of the whole Church. It is an eschatological concept, that is, it will only be fully completed at the consummation of all things when humanity is taken into perfect communion with God. This organic understanding is thus not juridically bounded by the authority of bishops. Instead, the ministry of the episcopate expresses the communion of the Church and this is ultimately focused through the college of bishops with the pope as the head of that college. Tillard's organic approach has been highly influential in the development of a widely accepted ecumenical ecclesiology. Placed alongside the insights of Zizioulas, it offers clear indicators for patterns of authority not only within Anglicanism but in the movement towards the reality of a universal Church which embraces all traditions. It is communion itself, both with God and by the grace of God among the faithful. This will support an organic and healthy exercise of authority that allows an appropriate distinctiveness within the local Church and a true respect and interdependence between eucharistic communities across the world.

Sign, instrument and foretaste?

We have already hinted at the 'unfinished' nature of the Church's ministry, which is itself a sharing in the ministry of Christ. This is most effectively reflected in seeing the ministry of the Church sacramentally. In describing the Church sacramentally we are driven back again to the sacraments themselves which point to the future consummation of God's kingdom. In speaking of the Church in this way ARCIC II noted: 'The sacramental nature of the Church as sign, instrument and foretaste of communion is especially manifest in the common celebration of the Eucharist.' Again reflecting Tillard's doctrine of the Church, the document continues: 'Here, celebrating the memorial of the Lord and partaking of his body and blood, the Church points to the origin of its communion in Christ, himself in communion with the Father.' Both the horizontal and vertical dimensions of communion are highlighted.[13]

In this same document, the interdependence of the local and universal are also focused. Both discipleship and common faith are required of each Christian, and what is true of the individual is equally true of the local Churches. Communion with other local Churches is essential to the integrity of the self-understanding of each local Church, precisely because of its catholicity. In the same paragraph the agreed statement goes on to say:

> Amid all the diversity that the catholicity intended by God implies, the Church's unity and coherence are maintained by the common confession of the one apostolic faith, a shared sacramental life, a common ministry of oversight, and joint ways of reaching decisions and giving authoritative teaching.

Although this document is intended as one further step along the path towards unity between two different communions, it is effectively addressed also to the two separate Churches, as they exist at present. Can Anglicanism boast that internationally at present there exist effective 'joint ways of reaching decisions and giving authoritative teaching'? How effectively does it manifest the catholicity which is a mark of the Church locally and universally?

The commission was not denying the possibility and even the virtue of diversity, but it was undoubtedly pressing home the need for a true and shared communion. For all the local Churches to be *together in communion*, a visible communion which is God's will for the Church, the criteria which underpin that communion must be both fulfilled and recognised in each of the separate but interdependent local eucharistic communities. It is by this means that visible communion is effected. We have already noted the nature of these criteria. ARCIC II accepts that 'This does not necessitate precisely the same canonical ordering: diversity of canonical structures is part of the acceptable diversity which enriches the one communion of all the Churches.'

The impact of the argument in this agreed statement will be significant for Anglicans if it is taken seriously. A variety of different issues have underscored the problems which arise if we do not continue to nurture communion. In some provinces, dioceses have raised questions about the lay celebration of the Eucharist. But what does this say about Church order and, indeed, about the historical commitment of Anglicanism to the threefold ministry of bishops, priests and deacons within the celebration of the Eucharist? The ordination of women to the priesthood (and to the episcopate in certain provinces) has led to impaired communion both between and even within provinces. Disagreement about some ethical issues – the Church's response to homosexual people is one example – also threatens to drive provinces apart from each other.

The image of the family is all too frequently used cloyingly and simplistically of the Church on the local level. It is, however, a useful image to employ here if we allow it to extend even to the most difficult relationships within family life. In the Western world, family life has been notoriously threatened in recent years both by divorce, and by the reluctance of many to enter into a marriage contract from the start. Divergence in understanding and belief between different generations has further threatened the fabric of family life. The message is that, far from being the source of eternal 'happy' relationships, human families can be the locus of bitterness, rancour and breakdown. For families to prosper there is at the very least a requirement of forbearance, of continuous conversation and respect for the other people while still recognising true interdependence. If one personality is allowed to dominate then there will result either the totalitarianism of the husband or wife or the collusion of those who will not face conflict. Conflict and disagreement cannot be avoided in relationships. The key to cherishing relationships is respect and sensitivity in managing conflict and disagreement.

This image of the human family is powerful in our understanding of the Church. Both history and theology indicate that the local and universal are essential ingredients within any healthy ecclesiology. They are also essential components to be balanced in any attempt to arrive at an effective pattern and structure of authority in the Church. Forbearance and a true recognition of interdependence are of the highest significance. In this way the Church mirrors elements within human family relationships. Within Anglicanism, the development of a worldwide communion was not the result of a conscious and coherent process of planning. History has already taught us that. On occasion, the shape of particular provinces was fashioned by a conscious desire to break away from the tyranny of the colonial relationship. In other cases the doctrine of the Church has emerged either from reaction against an earlier dominant Protestant or Catholic pattern or, indeed, it has derived from the founding fathers who had been formed in one of those traditions. Similarly, cultural and geographical factors help to determine priorities for provinces in the present day. In many developing countries, the ordination of women is at present either not an issue or it is culturally abhorrent. In other provinces where Anglicans are scattered thinly and clergy are few, issues of lay celebration take on a new significance. How should these questions be addressed?

The ecclesiologies of both Tillard and Zizioulas effectively begin with the reality of the local Church. That reality, however, gains its essential nature from the fact that each local Church is a eucharistic community and as such is focused in the celebration of the Lord's Supper where classically the bishop presides. It is this structured ministry which relates the community to the whole body of Christ both in space and time. Communion on this basis requires some sort of understanding of apostolic succession. It also requires collegiality and thus interdependence across cultures and geographical divides. Even our brief excursions into history, either within the New Testament or in the specific case of the Celtic and Roman missions to England, suggest something very similar. The collision of Celtic and Roman patterns of polity at Whitby in 664 should not be seen simply as a conflict with one assured victor. The Celtic mission itself made its way via Rome. Its distinctiveness was fashioned by the local, but its orthodoxy and common ground with the rest of Christendom showed a respect for the universal. Similarly, the Roman pattern would take on a different character relating to time and place. In France, Gallicanism is not dead. In Italy, the Milanese rite lives and thrives still in Milan and its environs. The local is not disavowed or driven underground.

Recent years have seen in international politics the growth of an extraordinary paradox. In Europe and, indeed, worldwide (Australia and the Pacific Rim is another example) there has been an increasing realisation of our interdependence. European nations believe that they can no longer survive economically (and probably politically) as isolationist nation states. The growth of the European Union is at least as much about political realities as it is about altruistic idealism. At the same time, however, there has been once again a vigorous rebirth of nationalism. It is not only the liberation of Eastern Europe and the fragmentation of the Soviet Union. In Italy the Liga Norda sue for self-government or even independence. In the United Kingdom, Scottish Nationalists continue to argue that independence is at the top of their agenda. Political reality lies in accepting elements of both these movements. Regionalism and nationalism affirm the importance of the local. European unity accepts the need for a true recognition of interdependence and the existence of universal needs.

It is not by accident that in these pages we moved towards an engagement with ecumenical theological dialogue. For we cannot begin to make sense of authority within Anglicanism if we do not place Anglicanism within the context of the universal Church and within the context of eternity. Will whatever authority structure we explore simply be for the benefit of Anglicans alone, or is it part of a journey of discovery that ultimately sees the destination as a universal Church expressing the communion of all local Churches with the triune God whose ministry we share and whose gospel we proclaim?

ᜍᜓ 6 ᜌᜓ

Anglicanism and the Universal Church

Eccentric Anglicanism

'There are no Anglicans in Sarajevo.'[1] This, Adrian Hastings informs his reader, was the response of a Lambeth Palace spokesman to the suggestion that, following a controversial visit to the Sudan, the archbishop of Canterbury should have visited war-torn Bosnia. There is no evidence to suggest that a spokesman actually uttered these words. Indeed, it is most unlikely that they were ever spoken, since the claim is manifestly untrue. Although the numbers may have been very small, there continued to exist a tiny Anglican community in Sarajevo throughout the bitter years of war. Hastings' rhetoric does, however, point towards a truth at a deeper level. If Anglicans were reticent in pontificating on the Yugoslavian war, was that not partly due to the fact that Anglicanism is not 'endemic' in those countries?

This is not the place to engage in the complex debate about whether or not the Church of England (or the Anglican Communion) should have taken a higher moral profile on the Yugoslavian crisis. This rhetorical exchange does, nevertheless, say something about the place of Anglicanism within Europe and in the wider world. Even a brief glance at a map of the European continent in the context of Christianity shows Anglicanism to be an eccentric phenomenon, an 'offshore operation' in comparison with other widespread Christian confessions. Not only are there few Anglicans in the Balkans, there are only tiny sprinklings of Anglicans (largely expatriates) in the rest of mainland Europe. Even within the United Kingdom and

Ireland, the vast majority of Anglicans are part of the Church of *England*. The Church of Ireland, the Church in Wales and the Scottish Episcopal Church are all minority Churches in their respective countries. In mainland Europe, Anglicanism is restricted to the diocese of Gibraltar in Europe, the Convocation of American Churches in Europe, the Spanish Episcopal Reformed Church and the Lusitanian Church in Portugal.

In the Netherlands, Germany, Switzerland and Austria there are Old Catholics who are in 'full communion' with the Church of England, but they are not 'Anglicans'. The same is true with regard to the Polish National Catholic Church. To complicate matters, there are also parallel Anglican jurisdictions in Europe. The Convocation of American Churches and the diocese of Europe both have bishops covering the same areas. In Spain and Portugal, alongside the congregations of the indigenous Anglican churches which have their own bishops, there are congregations which fall within the jurisdiction of the bishop of Gibraltar in Europe. All these anomalies raise questions about the universal aspects of Anglicanism and challenge orthodox understandings of catholicity. Anglicans are not, of course, the only Christians to be guilty of undermining the theology of episcopacy through the existence of parallel jurisdictions. In the previous chapter incidences of this same problem were given relating to both Roman Catholicism and Chalcedonian Orthodoxy.

How precisely does Anglicanism fit into the European scene? In March 1990, to celebrate and discuss the implications of the collapse of communism in Eastern Europe, a one-day gathering of European Church leaders was convened in Geneva by the Conference of European Churches (CEC) in association with the Conference of European Catholic Bishops' Conferences (CCEE). The archbishop of Canterbury played a key role in this meeting. The significance of his presence was enhanced, however, by him being the leader of a world communion (in Orthodox terms a patriarch) rather than by him being the primate of a dominant Church on the mainland European continent.

This point is further emphasised in a great meeting which takes place between the Churches throughout the European continent.

Those representing the mainland European Churches are used to the categories of Orthodox, Roman Catholic and Protestant. Furthermore, both Protestants and Roman Catholics are often keen, for different reasons, to place Anglicans under one of these two headings. Protestant solidarity and some common historical influences at the time of the Reformation understandably persuade the Protestant Churches that Anglicanism is at one with them. The break with the bishop of Rome is sufficient to persuade Roman Catholics too that Anglicans are Protestants. The Orthodox will rarely make this mistake. Anglican emphasis on the importance of the province, of the local Church, which parallels autocephaly in Orthodoxy; the continuation of the threefold ministry of bishop, priest and deacon; and the rooting of doctrine within Anglicanism in prayer and worship have clear resonances with Orthodoxy. So close are the parallels that in the mid-1930s the Romanian Orthodox Church recognised Anglican orders; it was only the failure of the Convocations of Canterbury and York to ratify this move that caused the recognition to be ineffective.

Anglican self-identity has always focused on the phrase 'Catholic but Reformed'. Continuity of the tradition, of orders of ministries and of sacramental patterns argue for catholicity. A rediscovery of Scripture, the compilation of vernacular and revised liturgical texts, and the significance of the lay voice through parliament are just some of the symbols of reform. Since the Reformation there have always been strong currents within the Church of England, and later within worldwide Anglicanism, which have emphasised claims to catholicity. Sometimes the evidence to support such claims has not been investigated entirely objectively; Anglo-Catholics have sometimes allowed special pleading to cloud clear theological judgement. History has been viewed through sacramentally tinted spectacles. Revisionist histories of the Reformation have taught us to be more circumspect here. The continuity of bishops in the 'historic sees', however, has been one further and significant plank in the argument that the Church of England is the 'catholic Church' of the land. Indeed, it is this same argument that has allowed a number of Lutheran Churches in the Nordic and Baltic countries to come together with the Anglican Churches in Britain and Ireland as one Church. The Porvöo Common Statement makes reference to this point on more than one occasion:

> The unbroken witness of successive bishops in the dioceses and the maintenance of pastoral and liturgical life in the cathedrals and churches of all our nations are an important manifestation of the continuity of Christian life across the ages, and of the unity between the churches in Britain and Ireland and in Northern Europe.[2]

And then later:

> At the time of the formation all our churches ordained bishops (sometimes the term superintendent was used as a synonym for bishop) to the existing sees of the Catholic Church, indicating their intention to continue the life and ministry of the One, Holy, Catholic and Apostolic Church.[3]

This is then translated into a more formal theological statement in the discussion of 'Episcopacy in the Service of the Apostolicity of the Church.'[4] The clear intention of the Churches who have signed the Porvöo Declaration is to become one Church, and to act as one Church through the exercise of joint episcopal oversight within Northern Europe. Presumably this will eventually have implications for the chaplaincies of the diocese of Gibraltar in Europe in the Nordic and Baltic countries. They will naturally fall under the jurisdiction of the bishop in whose diocese they are found. The implications of unity are a new appreciation of the nature and the ministry of the universal Church where in each place one bishop (possibly with a suffragan or assistant, although many would argue that suffragan and assistant bishops are a corruption of the theology of episcopacy) acts as the focus of unity for the Church. These moves described in Northern Europe are one model of understanding the relationship of Anglicanism to the universal Church of God. It remains, of course, only a partial unity until Roman Catholics, Orthodox and others can also be embraced and embrace one another within the universal Church.

The integrity of Anglicanism

The moves described above hint at a provisionality relating to the nature of the Church. The Church in Northern Europe post-Porvöo is effectively neither Anglican nor Lutheran. Admittedly in England Anglican polity will predominate, as in Norway, Estonia or Sweden Lutheran patterns will remain. The small Lutheran congregations in England, however, *will* be affected by these moves. What will be the effect upon 'confessional' Lutheranism? How can a confessional Church become one with another Church which appears worldwide to have a rather more pragmatic base? It is this sort of issue which has prompted a number of Anglican theologians to call upon the Churches within the Anglican Communion to pay more attention to ecclesiology. One of the most outspoken critics of Anglicanism's failure to address the doctrine of the Church is Bishop Stephen Sykes.

One of the fears of Sykes and other critics of Anglican ecclesiology is that other ecumenical partners cannot be clear about the nature of the Church with which they are in dialogue. Another related fear is that the Anglican Communion's authority will become so 'dispersed' that the communion itself will disintegrate. In his most popular exposition of these issues, Stephen Sykes heads his book[5] with a quotation from Thomas Hardy that puts all in context: 'There's this to be said for the Church [of England], a man can belong to the Church and bide in his cheerful old inn, and never trouble or worry his mind about doctrines at all.'[6]

A similar response comes to mind as I remember an encounter during a hospital visit some years ago. A young woman seemed to be appreciative of the visit but she was quick to define the extent of her Christian allegiance: 'Oh, I'm not religious or anything, I'm just Church of England.' This sort of response relates directly to Sykes's concern for the position of the Church of England, and thus by implication for Anglicanism more widely.

Sykes is keen to point out that the Anglican Communion is not an end in itself; it is no more than 'penultimate', but that nevertheless Anglicanism must be clear of its own doctrinal position for the sake of its own health, apart from anything else. Having established this point, he goes on to ask whether there is either 'an Anglican theology' or at the very least 'an Anglican method in theology'. The result of his discussion is to conclude with his own reflections on authority within Anglicanism. Sykes begins his argument by asserting that there are doctrines affirmed within the liturgical traditions of Anglicanism which over and again are central to Anglican self-understanding. Incarnational emphases are a case in point. How are understandings of the incarnation safeguarded such that they help constitute 'an Anglican theological approach'? A clear answer to this would help us to see how Anglicanism stands for a particular doctrinal position, even if that position has been patient of development within the history of the Church. Sykes moves on from this to argue that theological method is itself intrinsically related to the particular doctrinal position espoused. Hence, by implication, there is both an Anglican way of doing theology and a corpus of belief with an Anglican emphasis stamped upon it.

One of the points to which Sykes returns again and again is the failure of Anglicans to recognise the existence of any clear theological emphases within their tradition. This, he argues, is partially due to an avoidance of systematic theology. A clear emphasis upon systematic theology is further impeded by the lack of any great confession within the Anglican tradition parallel to the writings of Calvin or Luther. The earlier Anglican reliance upon the patristic tradition is difficult to defend now when making a broad overview of Anglican theological preoccupations in the present day. In other words, the Tractarian recalling of the Church of England to its patristic foundations no longer appears to be a major preoccupation within the Church. The theological community within English universities has furthermore not encouraged, or been enthusiastic in general to support, the serious development of a tradition of systematic theology. These weaknesses can hardly be denied, and they have undoubtedly contributed to the paucity of any sustained Anglican ecclesiology. Admittedly, a number of Anglican theologians have focused upon ecclesiological issues, and notable in this area would be the work of Charles Gore, Lionel Thornton, Eric Mascall and Michael Ramsey. While others could be added to this list it does

93

not constitute a consistent or clearly developing tradition. The tension and controversy between evangelicals, Tractarians and Broad Churchmen in the nineteenth century made the development of a consistent ecclesiological tradition difficult to sustain.

Theologically, then, there developed no clear ecclesiology. Empirically, as it were, the situation is rather different. At the time of the Reformation, Anglicans historically inherited the institutions of both episcopacy and the two dominical sacraments. The threefold ministry of bishop, priest and deacon has remained the backbone of Anglican structures of ministry, and there is thus inherently within the tradition an incipient ecclesiology. The interpretation of both episcopacy and sacramentality has, of course, varied. The conclusion of Sykes's argument on ecclesiology is this:

> The weakness of modern Anglican ecclesiology may be in part traced to the disrepute into which certain passionately held dogmas fell when exposed to historical criticism; but it must also be traced to the chronic reluctance of Anglicans to accept the fact that what they have inherited as institutions in the church unencumbered with sharply defined theoretical baggage has profound theological, especially ecclesiological, significance *as such*.

Most sharply of all he thus argues: 'it is only the theological exploration of the significance of such an inheritance which will begin to establish Anglicanism on lines significant for the future of the world-wide church'.[7]

Despite these harsh words, Sykes's thesis is certainly not purely negative. His coda on authority contrasts Anglicanism favourably with Roman Catholicism. One of the weaknesses of the documents of Vatican II, he argues, is their inability to comprehend how conflict in the Church is unavoidable. Indeed, some have suggested fairly harshly that the Roman Catholic Church does not itself find it easy to deal with conflict – it chooses between oppression and anarchy, often opting for the former. The Anglican pattern of dispersed authority realistically allows for this. In support of this he refers to an appendix to the 1948 Lambeth Conference Report which focuses on authority. The now classical Anglican understanding of 'dispersed authority' is set out there. Authority is both singular, deriving from the divine Trinity, and plural since it is distributed in numerous organically related elements. It is reflected, it is argued, in adherence to episcopacy as 'the source and centre of our order' and in the Book of Common Prayer. While Sykes accepts that this last point is left unargued, he nevertheless believes that this statement of Anglican authority has lasting value. Dispersed authority implies the existence of conflict.

Dispersed authority also implies that authority is not the possession only of the bishops or, indeed, the clergy. Sykes presses hard the point that the inclusion of laity within the councils of the Church is part of the distinctiveness of both Anglican ecclesiology and its pattern of authority. He puts it thus:

> it is of the essence of the Anglican view of authority that it should be maintained in principle that the means of judging matters concerning the faith are in the hands of the whole people of God by reason of their access to the Scriptures; and, further, that it is distinctively Anglican that this means is given to them in the liturgy of the church, backed by canon law.[8]

Finally, within this context is set episcopacy. Oversight must be seen within the wider understanding of the ministry of all Christian people. Sykes argues that 'In a broken church the episcopate which is the symbol of the continuity and integrity of the faith does not reside in any one person.'[9] In other words, the existence of more than one bishop in a particular region acknowledges the present divided nature of the Church. His instinct is thus to applaud the fact that, at the moment, Anglicanism has no sharply defined theory of episcopacy.

Confessionalism or provisionality

Anglicans have good reason for gratitude to Stephen Sykes in his rigorous critique of authority and ecclesiology. In the realm of authority he has made it clear that a bland reference to 'Scripture, tradition and reason' as the sources of authority for Anglicans simply will not do. The first two sources are common to all the mainstream Christian Churches. Furthermore, reason cannot be appealed to in itself as a source of authority. Sara Maitland makes this point cogently in a rather different context by stressing how the seventeenth-century Anglican divines who appealed to reason did not anyway understand reason as we now might understand it. It was not seen as the basis of an almost clinical process of clarifying the mind. Instead, it was intrinsic to Christian thought rather than an external application of attitudes of the mind. She quotes Bishop Jeremy Taylor:

> Reason is such a base of quicksilver that it abides nowhere: it dwells in no settled mansion; it is like a dove's neck, or a changeable taffeta; it looks to me otherwise than it looks to you who do not stand in the same light as I do. . . . The heart of reason, that vital and most sensible part, in which it can only be conquered fairly, is like an ambulatory essence and not fixed: it wanders up and down like a floating island, or like that which we call the life blood.

Maitland thus argues that reason as a concept in defining authority is less easily captured than many would assume.[10]

The application of reason is something which all the main Christian traditions would accept as essential, but reason cannot of itself be a source of authority. In terms of ecclesiology, Sykes requires of us a clearer analysis of Anglicanism's theological self-understanding. He is keen to contrast Anglican attitudes with those of Roman Catholicism and to support 'dispersed authority' as a concept.

Sykes is surely right, then, to require of Anglicans a firmer theological grip upon the traditions which they believe shape their communion. Dispersed authority takes the role of the whole people of God seriously, and it does justice to healthy conflict within the Church. The inherited historical traditions of the Western Church within ministry and the sacraments are an essential part of Anglican polity, but the need for a systematic theological analysis is equally important. There are, however, points where there appear to be internal inconsistencies within Sykes's argument. Although he is happy to argue generally for a clearer theological understanding of ministry, 'only the theological exploration of the significance of such an inheritance . . . will begin to establish Anglicanism on lines significant for the future of the world-wide church.' When it comes to episcopacy, he is happy for the theological understanding to remain vague: 'For this reason I believe it is a matter of considerable wisdom that the present Anglican episcopate is unencumbered with any sharply defined theological theory.'[11]

Admittedly, this allows for the provisionality not only of Anglicanism but of all the Churches; the implication is that theologians from different Churches may work together towards a theory of episcopacy that is supportable within the 'universal Church' of the future. This approach does, however, undermine the more general point that Anglicans need a clearer grasp of systematic theology and also a better theological analysis of the nature of the Church. Nevertheless, in essence Sykes's reflections upon polity and theology take seriously the need for a clearer corporate self-understanding if Anglicans are to make a substantial contribution to the modelling of a future united Church. The provisionality of Anglicanism is accepted, but the character that has developed over four and a half centuries and the need for a theology which reflects this are equally not ignored.

There still remain questions to his overall thesis, and these are at two levels. The first is a nagging fear that the weaknesses of patterns of theology and authority have not been finally answered. The second is the danger of giving Anglicanism such a clear sense of identity that the provisionality required by ecumenical dialogue is easily undermined. The 'loose ends' already noted in regard to episcopacy, combined with the need for more work on the nature of dispersed authority and of the role of the laity in the authority structures of the Church, need to be tied up. Present instruments of authority worldwide (the Primates' Meeting, the Lambeth Conference and the Anglican Consultative Council) all acknowledge the concept of dispersed authority, but is it dispersed beyond the recognition of any real authority? These organs also embrace the role of the laity in decision-making, but the precise nature of this role remains undefined and even inconsistent. Are there certain aspects of the Church's work where it is appropriate that the bishops retain and exercise authority? How should the doctrines of the Church be reflected upon and taught, and what should be the process for liturgical revision? This final question is profound in a Church which boasts that its theological self-understanding issues from its worship and its prayer. Consultations between Episcopal Churches may be the first step towards offering a model for episcopacy that may be held in common by all traditions, both Eastern and Western.

The second-level question relates to Anglicanism's self-identity. This is the point at which Sykes's antagonists most frequently dissent from his analysis. The cherishing by Anglicans of the doctrine of the incarnation (an argument stressed by Sykes) cannot be denied. Is this sufficient, however, to mark off Anglicanism as having a separately defined corpus of belief? The incarnation lies central to all Christian theology and spirituality; Anglicans have no monopoly here. It can reasonably be argued that certain Anglican theologians have contributed distinctively to our understanding of the incarnation – F.D. Maurice, Charles Gore and Michael Ramsey are but three good examples. Similar claims could be made, however, for theologians within other Christian Churches and confessions.

Elsewhere, Sykes rightly points within Anglicanism to the lack of seminal theological figures who could have offered a confessional seed around which a more distinctive ecclesiology might grow. Calvin's *Institutes*, and the *Augsburg Confession* and *Book of Concord* offer to the Reformed tradition and Lutheranism respectively precisely this. There is an undoubted clarity about both these traditions that manifests itself clearly in ecumenical dialogue. It is partly this which helped fashion both the concordat between Anglicans and Lutherans in the USA,[12] and also the Porvöo Common Statement. In the Porvöo Statement at least one of the chapter headings manifests clearly Lutheran confessional concerns on episcopacy when it is titled: 'Episcopacy in the Service of the Apostolicity of the Church.' Lutheranism is keen to preserve the notion of one single ministry within the Church of Christ, whereas the broader Western tradition has argued for a stronger emphasis on the threefold ministry of the Church.

As Sykes points out, there are no such documents within Anglicanism. The Thirty-Nine Articles are effectively a series of officially sanctioned tracts protecting the Church of England against, as it was then seen, the enormities of the Church of Rome. Such a document would be a negative starting-point for a confessional theology. The Book of Common Prayer, on the other hand, is the liturgical foundation of the Church of England and to some extent of Anglicanism worldwide. It is acknowledged to be the yardstick by which Anglicans measure doctrinal consistency, but it is not a confession. Both these documents are essential in understanding Anglicanism but they cannot be seen as the basis of a confessional theology.

If we are to preserve and protect the openness which Stephen Sykes sees as defining the penultimate nature of Anglicanism, then we would do well to avoid defining particular doctrines which are seen as distinctively understood within our own tradition. The inheritance of the threefold orders of ministry and of the sacraments suggests a different approach which affirms that Anglicanism is first and foremost a part of the Western Church. Such an approach would affirm the basic principles enunciated by Sykes: a commitment to systematic theology should remain and also a clear commitment to a theological explanation of the precise understanding that Anglicans have of these institutions. On this basis the emphasis would be on Anglicans spelling out their understanding of the Western theological tradition rather than carving out a separate 'confessional' self-identity. This would in itself clarify Anglican understandings of ecclesiology and the nature of authority. It would also indicate a profound dismay for the present proliferation of episcopal jurisdictions which manifest the divided nature of the Church. Among other things, it would require an Anglican critique of the theology of episcopacy. It might also avoid the danger of Anglicanism so further developing its institutions such that unity is deferred rather than advanced by an over-confessional understanding of its nature as Church.

Inspire continually the universal Church

With the development of Anglicanism worldwide, it is easy to view concern for the Church universal as a relatively modern phenomenon, aided and abetted by the growth of ecumenical dialogue. At the heart of the 1662 Book of Common Prayer, however, at the beginning of the 'Prayer for the Church', precisely this same understanding is there: 'We humbly beseech thee most mercifully to receive these our prayers which we offer unto thy Divine Majesty; beseeching thee to *inspire continually the universal Church* with the spirit of truth, unity and concord.' More fascinating still is that this phrase in the prayer is there from 1549 onwards. In the 1549 Prayer Book, the 'Prayer for the Church' is part of the Canon of the Mass, the Eucharistic Prayer, and so at the very heart of the liturgy. The sense of each worshipping congregation being part of the Church universal goes back to the beginning of Anglicanism. Indeed, it was again part of the inheritance of the great Western tradition reaching back through the Middle Ages, beyond 1054 and the Great Schism, to the one united and truly universal Church. That Church also included, of course, originally the Church triumphant and the saints in heaven, and not only 'Christ's Church militant here in earth' as immortalised in the 1662 Prayer Book. The words 'universal Church' reflect the phrase 'Catholic Church' in the earlier Western rite.

With the English roots of Anglicanism it is easy to assume that universality has always been a concept for which ecclesiologists have had to fight. Even a brief and cursory historical survey, however, undermines such an assumption. Cranmer's compilation of a vernacular liturgy was heavily dependent upon the work of the reforming Spanish cardinal, Francisco de Quiñones, and of the Reformed scholar Martin Bucer of Strasbourg (who later became regius professor of divinity at the University of Cambridge). The work of the Christian humanists, and particularly of Erasmus of Rotterdam, was influential throughout sixteenth-century Europe. Similar reflections could be made about the wide influence of Thomas Aquinas, William of Occam, Duns Scotus and the other philosophical 'schoolmen' of the thirteenth and fourteenth centuries.

Theology was often more European and universal during the medieval period than it has sometimes been during the modern era.

Reference has already been made to the journeys of both St Wilfrid and of Benedict Biscop in the seventh century to Rome. Wilfrid spent time at Lyons, and there was a real sense of cross-fertilisation through Wilfrid's ministry both in England and in mainland Europe. The missionary work of St Erik and St Henry, in Sweden and Finland respectively, began from Britain, as indeed did Boniface's work in Germany (Boniface was born at Crediton in Devon). The story is the same of many of the early missionaries, Celtic and Roman alike. Gregory the Great initiated Augustine's great missionary journey from Rome through France and finally to Canterbury. St Felix, missionary to East Anglia, was a native of Burgundy. St Paulinus of York was also sent by Pope Gregory to reinforce the Augustinian mission. From the Celtic tradition, the voyages of St Brendan are legendary in both senses of that word. St Willibrord went from Britain to the Low Countries, and St Columbanus started out from Ireland to set up his monastery at Bobbio on the Franco-Italian border. Judgements on the European nature of Christianity ought not to be based upon the all too frequent outbursts of English xenophobia in the late twentieth century.

In the early and later Middle Ages, then, the sense of the universality of the Christian Church was very strong, even after it had expanded into the far north-western extremities of Europe. It remained, of course, largely European, apart from the Christian Churches of Malabar and the Churches of the Caucasus, Ethiopia and North Africa. Even so, before the later schisms and pre-eminently before the Reformation, the intercourse between different parts of the Church, and notably in the West, was considerable. The background of Anselm before he became archbishop of Canterbury is a case in point. Born in Aosta in north-western Italy, he became a monk at the Benedictine abbey of Bec in Normandy and from there he followed Lanfranc as archbishop in the Benedictine foundation in Canterbury. In his struggles with William II, Anselm's European journeys continued as he travelled in and out of exile and pressed his claims with the pope.

101

The earliest roots of Anglicanism, then, spring from a clear appreciation of the Church universal and from the English Church being part of the wider Western tradition. The healthy independence of many local European traditions from earliest times, including the Milanese, the Gallican and Celtic rites, preserved an appropriate tension rooted in a cherishing of the local without forsaking the universal. The growth of Anglicanism in the past two centuries into a worldwide communion has rekindled the significance of the universal Church, but within a very different context. Anglicanism itself is now present in a vast range of different cultures. More than 30 provinces now exist, all in communion with the see of Canterbury, all recognising a primacy of honour in the archbishop of Canterbury, but all retaining autonomy as local Churches.

The issue of local and universal is then represented on two fronts, both within and beyond Anglicanism. As we further explore questions of authority, both these fronts will remain paramount. How should Anglicanism develop an authority structure that requires each local Church to take account of its sister Churches in communion with the see of Canterbury, without denying the reality and importance of its own local culture and needs? How can that same Church be nourished both by the wider Church and by other traditions, and also offer to the universal Church a theological understanding which will enrich ecclesiology and patterns of authority in the Christian Church universally? These are the questions that make multilateral ecumenical dialogue an imperative and not a luxury. What have we learnt, and can we still learn from such dialogue? When people question the relevance of ARCIC, at a time when unity between Anglicans and Roman Catholics still seems fairly distant, this must be the most immediate response. ARCIC may be the most potent instrument in helping both Anglicans and Roman Catholics to be more self-critical. It may, indeed, also offer some positive models for a future united and universal Church.

✍ 7 ✎

No Abiding City

Communion – across and within time

Suddenly, for no reason at all, my *Doubts* began. . . . Yes, I've
not known an hour's real happiness since. You see, it wasn't the
ordinary sort of Doubt about Cain's wife or the Old Testament
miracles or the consecration of Archbishop Parker. I'd been
taught how to explain all these while I was at college. No, it
was something deeper than all that. *I couldn't understand why
God had made the world at all. . . .* Once granted the first
step, I can see that everything else follows – Tower of Babel,
Babylonian captivity, Incarnation, Church, Bishops, incense,
everything – but what I couldn't see, and what I can't see now,
is *why* did it all begin?[1]

So writes Evelyn Waugh with his usual irony. But, as always, there
is much seriousness contained within his black humour. One of the
essential lessons contained there relates to what the second Vatican
council described as the 'hierarchy of truths'. The Tower of Babel,
incarnation and incense may not be precisely on the same level, but
the ultimate question of the meaning of creation relativises virtually
everything else. In that context, issues of the ordering of the
Church's life and its structures of authority do not assume prime
significance. They appear as second-order issues. Yet still further
beneath Waugh's ironic text lies an assumption that the Church,

bishops and even the consecration of Archbishop Parker are certainly of some significance.

Waugh's reflections are a good place from which to begin to reflect upon a theology of the Church. Reference to Matthew Parker's consecration reminds us of Anglicanism's insistence that its sacramental ministry stands within the continuing stream of apostolic succession. We have already noted the continuity which has allowed Anglicanism to be described as a form of reformed Western Catholicism. Adherence to the Catholic creeds, the first four ecumenical councils, the ministry of bishops, priests and deacons and the administration of the sacraments are all marks of the universal Church which Anglicans continue to embrace. The inheritance of the historic Catholic episcopal sees in England from the Reformation onwards is used as the starting-point in the Porvöo Common Statement for a sophisticated argument on episcopacy and apostolic succession.

This argument is based upon the belief that apostolicity must be rooted in the apostolicity of Churches. Discussions of the validity of and continuity in ministry should no longer begin with the orders of individual bishops, priests and deacons.[2] A pure 'pipeline' theory that simply attempts to trace an unbroken line of laying on of hands down the ages is inadequate in itself. It is also impossible to prove conclusively from the historic evidence available within any one Church. Nevertheless, the laying on of hands in ordinations to these three orders remains an essential *sign* of apostolicity. This is one of the reasons why, for example, since the Bonn Agreement in 1931 between the Church of England and the Old Catholic Church of the Union of Utrecht, mutual consecration has been practised. Mutual consecration has also been essential to the reunion schemes in the Indian subcontinent, and it is a hallmark of Porvöo too. It is in that sense that the consecration of Archbishop Parker remains of significance, while no longer being an ultimate test in the continuity of ordinations.

The issue of apostolicity has in the history of the Church been directly linked to authority. It is a bishop's claim to be part of a continuous apostolic line, tracing its roots to the early Church and then theoretically to the apostles, that forms part of the basis of his authority. It is that element of episcopal ministry that is rooted in 'diachronic communion', that is, communion across time and across the centuries. Equally important from earliest times for both the validity of orders and for authority in the Church is 'synchronic communion', communion within time, or communion within the experience of the contemporary Church, communion across geographical and thus continental boundaries. Throughout Christian history apostolicity has been guaranteed by communion between the bishops of the 'Catholic Church'. Bishops must be in communion with each other across the world.

The significance of the first ecumenical council at Nicaea in 325, then, was that it gathered together and so identified the Catholic Church. Those bishops who met in communion with each other were the apostolic representatives of the Church of their day. The intention of ecumenical councils has been to bring together representatives of the One, Holy, Catholic and Apostolic Church, and through such councils to define the expression of Christian faith. The statements promulgated by ecumenical councils then became authoritative for the Church; they are part of the structure and pattern of authority, hence reference in declarations of assent to such statements as 'the Catholic creeds'. It is, then, the gathering together of the Church in this way which offers a pattern of authority extending beyond the local Church and which holds Christian people together in communion. Thus, to effect this within Northern Europe, the Porvöo Declaration notes:

> We commit ourselves:
> ... to establish appropriate forms of collegial and conciliar consultation on significant matters of faith and order, life and work;
> ... to encourage consultations of representatives of our churches, and to facilitate learning and exchange of ideas and information in theological and pastoral matters.[3]

The second Vatican council, and the subsequent synods of bishops within the Roman Catholic Church, have sought to achieve similar aims. The Lambeth Conferences, the Primates' Meetings and the Anglican Consultative Council offer similar patterns of consultation within the Anglican Communion. Other world communions arrange general consultations. The Lutheran World Federation, for example, meets in conference increasingly regularly, and the Chalcedonian Orthodox Churches are beginning to re-establish patterns of consultation which extend beyond the boundaries of one individual patriarchate and autocephalous Church.

It is essential to differentiate, however, between the gatherings described above and the early ecumenical councils. Since 1054, at the latest, when the great schism occurred between the Eastern and Western Churches, no council has been truly ecumenical. Admittedly, the Council of Florence, from 1438 to 1445, attempted to reunite the Greek Church with the Catholic West, but ultimately this broke up in disarray with the Orthodox refusing to ratify the union between the Latins and the Greeks. All later councils and synods have been partial. Roman Catholicism has claimed the title ecumenical for other meetings, including Vatican II, but they would not be so recognised either by Orthodoxy or by the other Churches of divided Christendom. This situation focuses precisely one of the most profound issues of authority facing all the Christian Churches today: What does authority mean in a divided Church?

The Lutheran World Federation, in the past, would not have claimed for its international gatherings a significance which implied that their conclusions were absolutely 'binding' on the member Churches. It is interesting, however, to see how such international gatherings of Lutherans have increased in regularity and in their significance to member Churches. One might venture to argue that the international authority networks of Lutheranism are growing stronger and more formal. There is a developing sense of communion. Within Anglicanism, as we have already seen, the authority structures internationally have no binding power. Even the Lambeth Conference does not speak on behalf of the whole Church, or even on behalf of the bishops in communion with the see of Canterbury. It is a meeting of bishops which is consultative in nature. A similar point could be made in relation to the Primates' Meeting. Certainly both these bodies are taken seriously by the separate provinces, but decisions cannot ultimately bind them. The Anglican Consultative Council has even less sway upon decisions within an individual province. It has largely acted as a gathering within which bishops, priests and laity can offer reflections upon the future course of the Anglican Communion.

It is this very looseness of structure that is increasingly leading to questions about the nature of 'communion' and 'authority' within Anglicanism. At the 1988 Lambeth Conference it was the ordination of women that raised the thorniest problems of authority and communion. As the president of that conference, Robert Runcie, then archbishop of Canterbury, called for a reappraisal of the notion of the absolute independence of provinces and asked instead that Anglicans might begin to take more seriously 'interdependence'. The result of this plea was the establishment of a commission (later styled the Eames Commission after its chairman, Archbishop Robin Eames of Armagh) to report precisely on the relationship between communion and women in the episcopate within worldwide Anglicanism.[4] Also set out at that same conference with clarity were four 'embodiments' or 'agents' of unity, these being the archbishop of Canterbury, the Lambeth Conference, the Anglican Consultative Council and the Primates' Meeting. These are, of course, the instruments of communion that we have already encountered and the simple reaffirmation of the importance of these within a Lambeth Conference is not in itself enough. Although that conference (and particularly the leadership of the archbishop of Canterbury within it) achieved more in safeguarding unity within Anglicanism than almost any believed possible, the questions have not gone away, and pre-eminently this is true in the realm of ecumenical relations.

Ecumenical uncertainties

In his opening address to the 1988 Lambeth Conference, 'The Nature of the Unity We Seek', Robert Runcie spelt this out clearly: 'Another reason for looking critically at the notion of the absolute independence of provinces arises from our ecumenical dialogues with worldwide communions. These require decision and action at more than provincial level.'[5]

One of the complaints that has been levelled at Anglicans by ecumenical partners relates precisely to this. The complaint is that 'we do not know with whom we are conducting dialogue, nor indeed what is the status of an agreed statement'. If, despite the Lambeth Quadrilateral and the Final Report of the first Anglican–Roman Catholic International Commission, the diocese of Sydney can still contemplate lay celebration, what does that really say about Anglicanism's commitment to the threefold ministry of bishops, priests and deacons and an orthodox understanding of the two dominical sacraments and the sacramentality of the Church? Is the ecumenical agreement which has been hammered out merely an agreement among 18 or 20 scholars? Is it merely an agreement between a certain constituency within Anglicanism that takes these marks of catholicity seriously? Or is such agreement something that will eventually be ratified by provincial synods and then brought together in a common focus by international instruments of communion within Anglicanism? Is it truly something that is owned by the communion as a whole? Certainly, the 1988 Lambeth Conference welcomed the agreed statements and appended elucidations. It asked for some further work in the area of authority on Scripture and tradition, and on primacy and collegiality, but the response was one of broad acceptance.

It is, of course, in dialogue with the Roman Catholic Church that such questions have been raised most sharply. Its highly central-ised organs of authority make Roman Catholics feel suspicious when they see the degree of latitude within Anglicanism, and now also the existence of 'impaired communion' between Anglican provinces and even within provinces. Different arrangements have been agreed in different provinces to respond to difficulties caused by the decision to ordain women. Within the Church of England, for example, great care has been taken to try to preserve unity following the decision in November 1992 to ordain women to the priesthood. The centre-piece of this process has been the consecration of so-called 'provincial episcopal visitors', bishops who are entrusted with the sacramental care of those who are opposed to the ordination of women and who find themselves in impaired communion with their own diocesan bishop. The diocesan remains the bishop with jurisdiction over those parishes, but episcopal sacramental ministry is provided by one of the provincial episcopal visitors.

Such an approach has its attractions. It has signally avoided the emergence of 'no-go dioceses' where the priestly ministry of women would have been excluded. It has avoided, too, the division of dioceses into fragmented jurisdictions where even the appointment of a new priest in a parish would have slipped from the grasp of the diocesan. It has, however, led to the existence of the so-called 'two integrities'. Presumably the root of this term lies in the belief that within the one Church two different views over the ordination of women may be held *with integrity*. Practically, it has led to something which is more paradoxical, if not contradictory. It has led to islands of dissent and disagreement which effectively impair communion between the Anglicans of one parish with those of another. The root meaning of integrity as set out in the *Shorter Oxford English Dictionary* is: 'The condition of having no part or element wanting; unbroken state; material wholeness, completeness, entirety.' In other words, theologically the word 'integrity' could quite easily be stood in parallel to the term 'catholicity'. The existence of two integrities thus appears to deny the very essence of what integrity implies.

A number of Roman Catholic commentators have been dismayed by this move, preferring the honesty of a situation where the entire Church of England embraced a polity which allows for the ordination of women to the priesthood. Such commentators would allow that such a move would still have serious ecumenical implications. Nevertheless, it is argued, the ecumenical damage has been done by allowing women to be ordained as priests, and the existence of two groups within one Church in impaired communion with each other compounds the ecclesiological confusion. It can, of course, be argued that any 'development' within Christian doctrine or practice will require time before it is accepted by all. There is bound to be a period of *reception*, as this process has been called. This will ineluctably require the existence of anomalies for at least a limited period of time. The question that remains is nevertheless one of authority. Can two apparently parallel apostolates exist alongside each other without undermining an appropriate authority of the Church? People on both sides of the divide over the ordination of women question the theological logic of two integrities.

The decision in a number of provinces of the Anglican Communion to ordain women to the priesthood, and more recently to the episcopate, has led to a rather different but related ecumenical difficulty. This is the question as to whether any one part of the Church of God has the authority to make such a decision and implement it alone, and outside the authority of an ecumenical council. The Roman Catholic Church has made known its hostility to such moves for more than 20 years, and stretching back to the pontificate of Pope Paul VI and his letter *Inter Insignores*.[7] The official communiqué of the archbishop of Canterbury's (Dr George Carey) meeting with Pope John Paul II on 25 May 1992 also made clear that the two leaders had discussed the ordination of women, and that should the Church of England go ahead this would constitute a serious new obstacle on the path to unity. It is interesting, of course, that some Anglican provinces had been ordaining women since 1976, but that it was only when the Church of England threatened this move that Rome stated her objections as fiercely. A similar response issued from the Moscow patriarchate of the Russian Orthodox Church and almost derailed the visit of the archbishop of Canterbury to the patriarch of Moscow in May 1993. The implication in both these cases is that Roman Catholicism and Orthodoxy see Canterbury effectively as the 'patriarchal see'.

More recently, further pronouncements from both Pope John Paul II and Cardinal Ratzinger have brought into question whether the Church on earth has the authority to engage with such questions at all. The implication is that the Church does not have the authority to reflect upon what are seen as eternal verities, truths which are an integral part of fundamental Christian teaching. This almost seems to affirm the line of Mr Prendergast in our opening quotation from

Evelyn Waugh, who assumed that incense, bishops and incarnation are all questions of the same order. This issue of the hierarchy of truths lies outside the scope of this book. Nevertheless (assuming that the ordination of women is an issue that may be debated by the Church militant), the proximate issue of whether decisions of this nature may be made by *one* part of the Church unilaterally is central to the discussion.

Put at its most extreme, it is argued that any significantly contentious issue relating to the dogmas of or ordering of God's Church can be decided only by a universal (catholic) ecumenical council. It is this argument that is forwarded when intermittently there is pressure to set a fixed date for Easter. Only an ecumenical council could decide this, and such a council would need to include the Orthodox. The point is then made that the convening of such a council is impractical to the extent of being unthinkable. Certainly, such an approach would rule out any immediate discussion of the ordination of women. It would also, however, have ruled out the Declaration of Papal Infallibility in 1870 at Vatican I and the Declaration on Marian Dogmas (an infallible statement made on this occasion not by a council but by the Roman pontiff). Neither of these decisions was truly ecumenical, nor indeed was Vatican I a council of the universal Church. It was a council only of bishops offering their allegiance to the bishop of Rome.

Ecumenical innovation

If the immediately previous argument were to be accepted in its entirety, then its implications both through general (ecumenical) councils and indeed ecumenical dialogue between the Churches would tend towards an entirely static model of the Church. Truly ecumenical councils have not occurred for almost a millennium. This means that such an approach implies a repudiation of any doctrine of development, a doctrine which implicitly has been accepted not only by Anglicans and the Reformed Churches, but also by the Roman Catholic Church institutionally. The two Declarations on Papal Infallibility and Marian Dogmas constitute

111

'developments', even if they are believed to be simply explications of what the Christian Gospel has always implied and what Roman Catholic Christians have effectively always believed.

If we allow for the unacceptability of such a static view of the Church and the Gospel, then the apparent irresponsibility of Anglicanism in allowing for development over the ordination of women begins to be seen in a rather different light. Anglicanism may itself be able to contribute something to this process of development. Part of this is possible through its own distinctive understanding of Church polity. Robert Runcie identified the issue at another point in his opening address to the 1988 Lambeth Conference. He notes:

> If we still have some things to learn about synodical government I also believe we have something to give to the Church of Rome. For me the major criticism of the Anglican–Roman Catholic International Commission must be its lack of emphasis on the role of the laity in the decision-making of the Church.[8]

It has already become abundantly clear, earlier in our argument, that the role of the laity in decision-making in Anglicanism is a seminal issue. Runcie's argument here is, however, by implication much more far-reaching, for the force of his argument is that international ecumenical dialogue has of itself an essential part to play in our modelling of a future united and truly universal Church. On one level this is simply to state the obvious, since the *raison d'être* of ecumenical dialogue is to bring about the existence in some form of one Church in Christ. It is that qualification 'in some form' which is crucial. For much of the time, ecumenical dialogue is seen in purely immediate instrumental terms. ARCIC, on this basis (and the same could be said of other similar bilateral dialogues), becomes insignificant, otiose or redundant if the prospect of unity between the two dialogue partners has slipped into a more distant future. Often is heard the cry, 'They may as well pack up ARCIC; they're not going to get anywhere now!'

Robert Runcie's argument, however, implies a more gradual, more subtle and more even-handed view of dialogue than is often

assumed. It is easy for either dialogue partners simply to see reconciliation in terms of one partner submitting to the other.
Certainly, that was the Roman Catholic approach to unity in an
earlier generation. It is also the slightly cynical view of Roman
Catholic attitudes still held by some Anglicans. Acceptance of any
form of primacy focused on the bishop of Rome is seen as submission. Put crudely, 'an ecclesiastical leopard' is no more capable
of changing its spots than is a political leopard. One evangelical
Anglican has made the point sharply recently:

> [I]t is not clear that the positive achievements of institutional
> ministry as it has actually functioned over two thousand years
> outweigh the fetters it has placed upon the Church. If it is too
> much to compare theologies of ordination to the emperor's
> new clothes, we might nevertheless suggest that the
> emperor's clothes are only too real, but you can see through
> them. As someone said about ARCIC and its defence of the
> papacy, we have to theologise about the actual popes, not just
> the theory.[9]

But that is to take an altogether far too cynical view of ecumenical
dialogue. First of all, ARCIC does not simply 'defend the papacy'.
ARCIC makes clear how significant developments in the Roman
Catholic Church have in themselves irrevocably affected the understanding and practice of papal authority. Despite recent attempts to
consolidate the power of the curia, debate cannot be stifled in the
Roman Catholic Church. Furthermore, this is in itself the beginning
and not the end of a process. The ordination of women to the
priesthood and even the episcopate is as much an issue for the
Roman Catholic Church as it is for Anglicans. Secondly, ARCIC
has acted as a mirror to Anglicans and Roman Catholics alike. The
papacy has been described more sharply in both its strengths and
its weaknesses. Precisely the same thing can be said of authority
within Anglicanism.

On this basis, perhaps the essential function of ecumenical dialogue at present is to act precisely in this way, as a mirror. It helps
us all as Churches to see ourselves as we really are and not as we

would like to be. Furthermore, it then presses us to imagine a Church which is neither made in an Anglican, nor a Lutheran, nor an Orthodox, nor a Roman Catholic image. Each of us will contribute to patterns of authority and practice which will mirror more truly the community that Christ would have us be. It will be made in his image, and it will be his ministry that we offer. Such an approach means that ARCIC and other ecumenical dialogues will have a profoundly relativising effect. There will be radical implications for each partner, and nowhere more so than in the realm of authority, for it is when authority is affected that we feel most threatened.

Paradoxically, some recent developments within Anglicanism have made us face these truths more sharply than before. It can hardly be denied that it is more rather than less satisfactory for individual (and relatively small) parts of the Christian Church to pioneer significant developments within the ministry of the Church unilaterally. But it is equally unsatisfactory for us to find our partners forbidding dialogue on just such issues, for that in itself implies either that one partner has a monopoly of the truth, or that Church and Gospel can only be understood statically. The debate over the ordination of women illustrates all too graphically the tragedy of Churches ignoring each other as they reflect theologically and practically upon the implications of the Gospel. The contradiction of *two integrities* within one Church stands in contrast to the equally profound contradiction enshrined in the belief that *the Church on earth does not have the authority* to reflect upon the way in which it orders its ministry.

No abiding city

The relativising efforts of dialogue (both theologically and on practical issues) between Churches argues for a new understanding of authority which corresponds to none of the models held at present by any of the Churches. Once again in his opening address to that 1988 Lambeth Conference, Robert Runcie implies just this:

But I want to say too that we must never make the survival of the Anglican Communion an end in itself, the Churches of the Anglican Communion have never claimed to be more than a part of the one holy catholic and apostolic Church. Anglicanism, as a separate denomination, has a radically provisional character, which we must never allow to be obscured.[10]

This approach is easily caricatured as either some form of ecclesiastical masochism and suicide, or as a thinly veiled version of 'crypto-papism'. Anglicanism, never having been sure of precisely what it is, defers to its larger and more powerful sister and submerges itself in a little-changed Western Church. But this is far from what Runcie and others intend by their argument. Essential to that last quotation are the words 'have never claimed'. Anglican self-understanding has been more subtle than is often assumed. To accept a provisionality is not to fall away from firmly held and argued beliefs; Runcie's earlier comments on the role of the laity in decision-making makes this plain. Other examples from Anglican self-understanding could be cited. Orthodoxy and Roman Catholicism have made more direct claims for their understanding of authority, but even here there has been a shift. The Vatican II claim that the Church 'subsists' in the Roman Catholic Church does not mean that the presence of the Church is 'exhausted', as it were, in an encounter with the Roman Communion. The Church Universal is not claimed as being identical with the Roman Catholic Church. This was what opened the doors of the Vatican to ecumenical dialogue.

It is almost certainly in the area of authority that the most difficult work is still to be done, both ecumenically and also in our wider understanding of the nature of the Church. Although in the sixteenth century there was profound disagreement about the nature of Christian ministry, the operation of the sacraments and the understanding of salvation, these issues in themselves are now less divisive. Agreement on the nature of the Eucharist was achieved fairly swiftly. The burgeoning of the liturgical movement and a rediscovery of common and complementary roots of Christian spirituality have allowed progress here to be consolidated.

Intercommunion has become more acceptable partly because there is a greater sense of Christians from different traditions having a common understanding of the nature of the Eucharist.

Similarly, understanding of Christian ministry is now shared to a greater degree. The relationship between the presbyterate and the priesthood of all believers has been spelt out. There has been developing a greater common understanding of the representative nature of Christian ministry, albeit a representative ministry rooted in the character of Christ. What is perhaps most interesting is that where there are still differences and divisions about either ministry or the Eucharist, these differences can often be traced back to disagreements about *authority in the Church* and how this is administered through the Church's ministers or how it is to affect the administration of the Church's sacraments. Interestingly, the roots of disagreement about the ordination of women to the priesthood and the episcopate can be traced most often to issues of authority. Who should decide? Has it happened before? (There has been less controversy, for example, about the ordination or women to the diaconate since there appear to be historical precedents for this in the early Church.)

If we believe the Christian Church to be the pilgrim people of God, then issues of authority will always be threatening for us, for the issues raised are of continuity and change, stability and innovation, tradition and a Church open to the future. Again, ecumenical dialogue has exposed this threat sharply. During his pilgrimage to Rome in 1989 in his meetings with Pope John Paul II, the archbishop of Canterbury opened up these challenges, building upon the foundations set out in the Final Report of ARCIC I. Standing in the Church of Saint Andrew and Saint Gregory on the Caelian Hill, the church on the site of the monastery from which Pope Gregory the Great had despatched Augustine to Canterbury, Pope John Paul first noted:

> It is my firm hope that our meeting in Rome will pave the way for the time when Rome and Canterbury will once more be fully able to proclaim together the 'word of truth' as they

did in the days of Gregory and Augustine. . . . The missionary task gives new urgency to our ecumenical endeavours.[11]

Following the pope's homily during vespers, the archbishop of Canterbury delivered an address, within which he reflected:

we are also discovering the need of wider bonds of affection. Gregory's example of a primacy for the sake of unity had mission – which we also see embodied in the ministry of his successor, John Paul II – which begins to find a place in Anglican thinking.

I tried to give voice to this at the last Lambeth Conference where I spoke of the need for a personal focus of unity. Within the Anglican Communion my own office is in part a response to this need. But for the universal Church I renew the plea I made at the Lambeth Conference: could not all Christians come to reconsider the kind of primacy the bishop of Rome exercised within the early Church, a 'presiding in love' for the sake of the unity of the Churches in the diversity of their mission?[12]

In many ways this is a model of how the Church might struggle to find an appropriate model of authority. Cynics will still see this as simply Anglican submission to the papacy, or indeed the submission of the entire Christian Church to the Roman curia. It is obvious, however, from the tenor and content of the archbishop's words, that his conclusions are just as challenging to the Roman Catholic Church as they are to Anglicans and other Christians, for he talks of 'the kind of primacy the bishop of Rome exercised within the early Church, a "presiding in love" for the sake of the unity of the Churches in the diversity of their mission'.

His reference to both a primacy of love and to diversity in unity imply a direct challenge to the jurisdictional and centralised models which still apply to the papacy at present. These same words challenge Anglicans to work for a more robust pattern of authority which requires an interdependence and an acceptance of our duty to our fellow women and men in other parts of the Church, and not purely to our own agenda and interests. This model of ecumenical dialogue, mirroring and challenging the present *status quo*, has immediate implications for proximate goals and patterns of authority in Anglicanism, and not only for the ultimate goals of the universal Church. What should it mean for the 'embodiments', 'agents' and 'instruments' of communion within Anglicanism? How can we arrive at more robust understandings of interdependence rooted in the teaching of Christ in the New Testament?

Authority and the Gospel

Reason and unreason

At the heart of so much of the ecumenical theological dialogue of
the past 30 years has been the issue of authority. Is authority too
centralised and dogmatic, or is it too dispersed and ineffectual? How
does authority relate to the tradition? What precise part does holy
Scripture play in offering a reasoned Christian pattern of authority?
Does an authority pattern which begins with Scripture immediately
imply a static and dogmatic system? Will such a pattern allow for
development and dynamism within the tradition? Starting from a
Roman Catholic standpoint, David Lodge asks similar questions.
He begins by reflecting on a rather different aspect of dogmatism.
In one of his novels he writes:

> How different it must be, he thought, the life of an ordinary,
> non-Catholic parent, free to decide – actually to *decide*, in calm
> confidence – whether or not to have a child. How different
> from his own married state. . . . While waiting, . . . he mentally
> composed a short article, '*Catholicism, Roman*', for a Martian
> encyclopaedia compiled after life on earth had been destroyed
> by atomic warfare: '*Roman Catholicism was, according to archaeo-*
> *logical evidence, distributed fairly widely over the planet earth in*
> *the twentieth century. As far as the Western Hemisphere is con-*
> *cerned, it appears to have been characterised by a complex system*
> *of sexual taboos and rituals. Intercourse between married partners*
> *was restricted to certain limited periods determined by the calendar*

and the body temperature of the female. . . . Other doctrines of the
Roman Catholics included a belief in a Divine Redeemer and in
a life after death.'[1]

David Lodge's parody of Roman Catholicism takes as its point
of departure the effects of authoritative teaching upon the life of
individuals and families. Dogma, in the realm of morals, impinges
directly on family planning in this case and suggests unthinking and
irrational patterns of authority. Lodge's reflections are a parody,
and Roman Catholic patterns of authority are infinitely more
subtle and well argued than this extract implies. Nevertheless, it is
undoubtedly the case that the jurisdiction and teaching authority of
the hierarchy is felt more directly by the laity than it is in other
Churches. It is also clear that there is an assumption that the
tradition will be received by both the clergy and the faithful without
too much question. Presumably it is just these attitudes that Lodge
is intent to pillory.

Within Anglicanism, precisely the opposite is often assumed to
be the case. Teaching on marriage and sexual ethics is assumed
to be lax or non-existent. Anglicans are assumed to concern themselves solely with liberty, to espouse an ethic which is unprincipled
and pragmatic, and to disregard the common good in their concern
for the individual. The ARCIC II Report on morals puts it thus:

> Anglicans, . . . while acknowledging the same ultimate values,
> are not persuaded that the laws as we apprehend them are
> necessarily absolute. In certain circumstances, they would
> argue, it might be right to incorporate contextual and pastoral
> considerations in the formulation of a moral law.[2]

Underlying this statement is an acknowledgement that the Anglican
approach to theological scholarship has generally been more exploratory and speculative than that of Roman Catholicism. Nowhere has
this exploratory attitude been clearer than in attitudes to biblical
scholarship. Here, Anglicanism has paralleled much more nearly
the approaches of Northern European Reformed scholarship, and
notably those of Lutheranism in Germany and Scandinavia. Atti-

tudes to the Bible are essential to any understanding of authority since the biblical record, as it issued from the earliest Christian community, in the first crystallisation of the 'tradition'.

It would be oversimplistic and simply untrue to contrast Anglican approaches to biblical scholarship with those of other Churches. There is within Anglicanism itself a wide variety of approaches, from fundamentalism in some conservative evangelical circles to extreme relativism in more radical circles. Furthermore, it would be unhelpful to single out the Bible as one prime source of authority. Such an attitude results in the *sola scriptura* approach favoured by some at the time of the Reformation. Even so, reflection upon the significance and interpretation of Scripture is essential to any understanding of authority in the Church, and it is apposite in this context to begin with Anglican scholarship and Anglican teaching on biblical authority. Before we do this, however, some further scene-setting is in order.

The strangeness of the Gospel?

Over the past 200 years a series of different tools (of a critical nature) have been fashioned for the study of biblical texts. Both historical and literary critical methods have been employed. These methods have enabled scholars to understand more clearly how the different books of the Old and New Testaments reached their present form. The narratives of the Pentateuch (the first five books of the Bible), for example, are now believed to be the product of a series of four or five writers or editors. The earliest text was worked upon by a series of later editors who added new material, and who also refashioned the texts taking into account the context of their own communities. Another insight was provided by the development of so-called 'form criticism'. Here the discovery was of a series of different literary forms or genres. This was pioneered with the Psalms. Different types or 'forms' of psalm were discovered, which included laments, penitential psalms, psalms from the ceremonies relating to the royal court and others. Within the gospels, too, different types of story were identified, including parables, miracle stories and controversy narratives.

In recent years a series of new critical methods has been developed. 'Redaction criticism' emphasises the fact that each book and each writer has its/his own theological style. The redactor or editor fashions the material, leaving the imprint of a distinctive theological slant. Sociological criticism has laid a new emphasis on the communities from which the different biblical narratives emerged. These different communities each have their own presuppositions and needs which help dictate the final form of the text. More recent literary critical approaches have stood back from the historical background of the various books and have instead analysed the literary nature of the texts as we now confront them. Such literary critical approaches have utilised a great variety of new tools generated in other disciplines, and, more recently, so-called 'structuralist' methods have often been used.

For many, this great variety of new tools has been liberating in the study and interpretation of the Bible; for some, it has been threatening. Whatever the response of either the individual or the community, critical study of the Bible requires a measured response from those who would interpret the Scriptures. Three particular challenges arise. First of all, naïve theories of inspiration can no longer be taken seriously. Few would now argue for a notion of inspiration whereby God dictated the text directly into the minds of individuals or on to the pages of the evangelist's codex. Instead, our understanding of inspiration must be more subtle; the human/divine interplay is complex, as indeed it is in daily life. Second (and closely related to this), interpretation is itself required to be more sophisticated. We cannot treat the Bible as if it is a rule book or a manual from which we can directly read off answers to the problems that we face in the contemporary world. Finally, the fact that the Bible came into existence over a period of more than a millennium suggests that there is inevitably considerable cultural diversity both within the Bible, and between the biblical texts as we receive them, and the contemporary world.

This final insight was most highly developed by a number of

scholars (and not only theologians) in what we might describe as the 'cultural relativist' school in the late 1960s and early 1970s. Pre-eminent in this school was the work of Dennis Nineham. Nineham argued for the inherent strangeness of the Gospel and the gospel world. The world of first-century Palestine is radically different from our own. In itself, this insight was not new. As early as the turn of this century, Albert Schweitzer had written: 'The historical Jesus will be to our time a stranger and enigma. . . . He does not stay; He passes by our time and returns to his own.'[3]

Some thirty years later, R.H. Lightfoot reflected:

> It seems, then, that the form of the earthly no less than of the heavenly Christ is for the most part hidden from us. For all the inestimable value of the gospels, they yield us little more than a whisper of his voice; we trace in them but the outskirts of his ways.[4]

There is no doubt that it is difficult, indeed impossible, for us to recover the historical Jesus in the way that we might recover some historical figures from a more recent age. Similar things might be said generally about the apostolic community. The historical evidence available to us is limited, and outside the New Testament there are only glancing references to Christ and virtually none to the earliest Christians. This does not, however, mean that we have no historical evidence. It simply means that our historical claims must be modest.

Nineham and his school, however, do not simply argue that the historical evidence is sparse. Their argument is that the entire cultural framework of the various ages of the Bible is built upon entirely different presuppositions from ours. Two or three examples will suffice to press home the point. In first-century Palestine, illness and mental instability were seen to be the result of demonic possession; there was no developed medical science as we know it. Secondly, the place of women was radically different from what it is now; it was unthinkable, for example, that women could have rights in matters of marriage and divorce, and Matthew corrects Mark on this issue when he takes over Mark's account as part of the basis of

123

his gospel. Thirdly, there are any number of problems that we face now that did not exist in New Testament times; nuclear weaponry and embryo research are just two such issues. Nineham effectively argues that the two cultures are so different that the radical strangeness of the gospel world makes it well-nigh impossible to use the Bible authoritatively in the present day.[5]

Part of Nineham's argument rested on the more profound philosophical assumption that cultures differ so radically from each other that one age cannot speak to another. To use a musical analogy that has been used before in this area, even if we construct 'original' eighteenth-century instruments to precisely the patterns we know they used, even if we follow the marking of the scores rigorously, and even if we read our way into the musical culture of the time, still we cannot know whether our conductors have really resonated with the past age nor whether we really have heard the music as they would have heard it. Nineham talks of world-views as 'totalities', entire constructs which frame a particular culture and its way of thinking.

Nineham's work was essential in directing us to the dangers in interpreting the Bible naïvely. It is not clear, however, that his arguments are watertight throughout. Do cultures really exist as totalities, for example? It is likely that some elements of a culture will stray into another age whereas other elements will not. Also, how total are totalities? Does an entire culture resonate on one unchanging note? Our fragmented contemporary culture suggests otherwise.[6] Indeed, if the relativist argument is taken to its ultimate conclusion then it is bound to suggest that individuals and cultures even *within* one particular age are incapable of mutual communication. We are all reduced to isolation within ourselves and ultimately to silence. Any understanding of the continuity of tradition within Christianity would vanish. The Gospel would remain entirely strange to all generations but its own.

We need, then, as we construct any authority rooted in tradition, to recognise the 'strangeness' of the Gospel. That, indeed, is part of its challenge to each succeeding age. We need also to take seriously the relativities which separate cultures and which require us to place the tradition in context. But we must recognise continuity between cultures if conversation within humanity is to continue and authority is not to disintegrate, allowing the growth of a fragmented and anarchic society. Nowhere is this clearer than in contemporary Christian attempts to respond to acute moral dilemmas.

The continuity of the Gospel

One of the most vexed ethical questions within the Churches today is the issue of homosexuality. Much ink has been spilt over the years on the subject and numerous reports have been published. It is a subject which engages all the issues relating to authority in the Church and authority in holy Scripture. Anglican reports have tried to take these issues seriously, often with controversial results. The 1979 General Synod Board of Social Responsibility Report for the Church of England noted of the Bible:

> First, the biblical writings certainly reflect the social ethos, needs and structure of a particular society or particular group at various stages of its development. We live in a society which is in many ways very different from anything to be found in the Bible and we are often able to see a degree of relativity in biblical attitudes and standards, in a way that was not possible to previous generations, in the light of historical, anthropological, sociological and psychological knowledge which was not available to them.[7]

Here the cultural relativists' point is made clearly in an official report to the Church. The report was savagely criticised, not least for its attitudes to biblical interpretation. It was argued that the discontinuities were emphasised at the expense of clear continuities. Furthermore, it was argued, the Gospel will at times challenge the prevailing mores of a society and that in itself is part of the function of the Gospel message. Patterns of authority, Christian and secular, will not always coincide or reinforce each other. In the light of these reflections, Anglicans have attempted to view the Bible in such a manner that there is made plain an authority that is both authentically Christian and offers signposts for each age. The Bible is an essential resource, but it must be handled with sophistication. We must not expect to read off 'ready-made' answers from the biblical text. Such a pattern of interpretation allows the tradition to 'inform' our contemporary deliberations rather than to dictate them. In a classic article on this theme, Michael Ramsey placed the locus of such an authority in the person of Christ rather than in the biblical text *per se*. Furthermore, he argued that the authority of Christ is mediated through word and sacrament within the Church. Thus this pattern of authority will be lived and will develop through the common life of the Church. This understanding was set out in a resolution of the Lambeth Conference of 1958:

> The Conference affirms that Jesus Christ lives in his Church through the Holy Spirit according to his promise, and that the Church is therefore both guardian and interpreter of Holy Scripture; nevertheless the Church may teach nothing as necessary for eternal salvation but what may be concluded and proved by the Scripture.[9]

Later, among the resolutions of the same conference, there is reference to the need for interpretation of the Bible in the light of modern thought in co-operation with scholars from other disciplines. There is also a call for imagination in interpretation and for an embracing of new translations of Scripture. In conclusion, there is a call for new and deeper study of the Bible.[10]

All these reflections emphasise the continuity of the authority of the Gospel as mediated through the Church. The Lambeth Conference resolutions do not underestimate the significance of modern scholarship. On the contrary, such scholarship and such interdisciplinary co-operation on the interpretation and authority of the Bible is encouraged. Scholarship is set within the context of the life of the Church. This is not intended to censor or to restrict the rigour and seriousness of that scholarship. Instead, it is intended to increase the sophistication of interpretation and understanding. In other words, it is not sufficient to apply various critical methods, almost in the style of a laboratory; our use of the Bible as an essential source of authority within the Church requires application. To extend the scientific analogy of the laboratory, biblical interpretation is a matter of both pure science and technology. The best of modern scholarship must be combined with the best methods of interpretation, a process which has more recently been given the technical name of *hermeneutics*.

This hermeneutical process is of significance to the whole Church of God and is not confined to debates within Anglicanism. Anglicans have engaged in a wider discussion of the authority of Scripture once again through the instrument of theological dialogue. In the statement on authority included within the Final Report of ARCIC I, the normative nature of the New Testament is set out clearly. The scriptural documents are described as 'the normative record of the authentic foundation of the faith'.[11] That same statement affirms that it is the Church which is responsible for creating a common mind for interpreting Scripture so that we may respond to its authority.

Responses to this statement called for even greater clarity and commitment to the place of Scripture. Consequently, the Elucidation of 1981 devoted a complete paragraph solely to this subject. The force of the argument there was to affirm the significance of both the Old and New Testaments. The centrality of the person of Christ, as in our earlier references to the work of Michael Ramsey, is a key element in the argument. The unique place of Scripture is affirmed, but once again within the context of the Church. The relationship of Scripture and tradition is more fully explored.[12] This area is one to which ARCIC II has returned in its most recent work. The differences between Anglicanism and the Roman Catholic Church on the ordination of women have made clear that the issue of authority in the Church and its relation to Scripture and tradition is perhaps the single most significant point of division.

Despite these continuing differences, enormous strides have been made regarding authority in the Church. There is good reason to believe that on the role of Scripture the two communions are now close to a common appreciation. The realisation within Anglicanism that authority is an issue of great significance has led the communion to look more carefully at the role of Scripture within the wider question of authority. The renewal of biblical scholarship within the Roman Catholic tradition has issued in a new and sophisticated treatment of this subject, and nowhere more so than in the recent document produced by the Pontifical Biblical Commission which bears the title *The Interpretation of the Bible within the Church*. After a careful analysis of different critical methods pursued with an exemplary clarity the writers note:

> Exegetes may have a distinctive role in the interpretation of the Bible but they do not exercise a monopoly. This activity within the church has aspects which go beyond the academic analysis of texts. The church, indeed, does not regard the Bible simply as a collection of historical documents dealing with its own origins – it receives the Bible as word of God, addressed both to itself and to the entire world at the present time. This conviction, stemming from the faith, leads in turn to the work of actualising and inculturating the biblical message, as well as to various uses of the inspired text in liturgy, in *lectio divina*, in pastoral ministry and in the ecumenical movement.[13]

This reflection resonates with the argument we have set out, and it is interesting to note how the English editor of the translation and the accompanying essays, himself a liberal Anglican, endorses the conclusions of the document. Critical scholarship is essential, but so is the context of the Church. We need to interpret and to understand the 'strangeness' of the Gospel in order that we may better appreciate its continuity.

Scripture and tradition

In post-Reformation times one of the continuing controversies between Catholics and Protestants was the relationship of Scripture to tradition. In their attempt to re-establish the fundamental importance of the witness of Scripture and its 'once and for all' nature, Protestants were keen to press for a clear distinction between Scripture and tradition. Roman Catholics, equally keen to stress the continuity of the Church and its authority, stressed the essential significance of tradition. This debate is one which has been central to ecumenical theological dialogue. It is not inaccurate to argue that, to a large extent, there has been a *rapprochement* which does justice to both emphases in both Churches.

The notion of tradition is one which issues from Scripture itself. The meaning of tradition is that which is 'handed on', and the Greek word for 'handing on' is a crucial term within the New Testament. It is the same word used of Jesus at his betrayal, but in that case it is translated as 'handed over'. One of the essential references to this process of handing on in the New Testament is in Paul's first letter to the Corinthians. In the passage relating to the resurrection in I Corinthians 15, Paul refers precisely to the activity of 'handing on'. In verses 3–4 Paul writes: 'For I *delivered* to you as of first importance what I also received, that Christ died for our sins in accordance with the scriptures, that he was buried, that he was raised on the third day in accordance with the scriptures.' The word *deliver* is that same Greek verb 'to hand on' or 'to hand over'. In this passage (and in the verses that follow) Paul sets out that which was handed over, that is, the essence of the Gospel, the tradition. Furthermore, that tradition itself is seen within the context of a greater continuity, since it is 'in accordance with the scriptures'. Elsewhere, Paul recites a similar formula in 1 Corinthians 11:23. 'For I received from the Lord what I also *delivered* to you, that the Lord Jesus on the night when he was betrayed took bread.' The passage here is, of course, the institution of the Eucharist. Again, it is an essential part of the tradition which is being 'handed on'.

Both these passages crystallise that which is at the heart of the Gospel, the essence of the tradition, that Jesus Christ was crucified and is risen. In one case it is a recitation of a 'credal formula', the basis upon which the Gospel is preached. In the other case it is an early liturgical tradition presumably outlining the living practice of the early Christian community. At the heart of the Christian life is the Eucharist. The tradition is brought to life and made real within the Church through the process of 'memory'. It is precisely the same process that has continued down the ages and which is at the heart of the Christian community at the present day. It is not simply a listing of beliefs and definitions, it is the Church repeating, refashioning, clarifying that which has been received. The Church is constantly called upon to translate and interpret the tradition within the relativities of each successive age and culture. In this, the process of memory and handing on is dynamic. Not only does it correct the Church where it might err, but it opens up new possibilities and implications of the Gospel for a new generation.

Paul's classic encapsulation of the tradition, then, and the process by which that tradition is proclaimed anew in each generation, sets tradition within the context of Scripture and by doing so clarifies the relationship of the two to each other. Scripture is not simply subsumed into tradition and through that into the authority structures of the Church. Instead, Scripture is determinative, inasmuch as it is the place where classically the Gospel is encapsulated in the events surrounding the ministry, crucifixion and resurrection of Jesus Christ. Scripture itself affords for us examples of how the Gospel is proclaimed anew in different contexts. We see how the earliest tradition is itself endowed with a dynamic. We see, too, how the tradition in successive generations stands in succession to Scripture, is consonant with it without somehow fossilising the Gospel. This pattern is essential to the continuing life of the Church and the generation of patterns of authority within it.

Guarding a dynamic tradition

Returning to a theme touched upon earlier, some five years ago the General Synod of the Church of England was constrained to respond once again to the moral issues raised by homosexual relationships. The response of the synod to the issues focused obliquely upon the question of authority in the Church. It was the House of Bishops that was called upon for an official response. The reasons for asking the bishops to reflect is well summarised in this brief quotation from the first paragraph of their report: 'In what follows we have tried, as those entrusted with guarding Christ's truth and caring for his people, to be faithful to what we have been shown of his mind.'[14]

In the report that followed, 14 out of 48 pages were specifically focused on biblical teaching. Thereafter the discussion continued to refer to this wellspring of the tradition. In expounding the scriptural witness on the subject the bishops believed themselves to be 'guarding Christ's truth' and being 'faithful to what we have been shown of his mind'. This clearly stands within the wider stream of thought within the Christian Churches which sees Scripture as delivering the Church from error. In an episcopally ordered Church the bishops are specifically required to guard the truth of the Gospel. Despite this overtly stated intention, the report was widely criticised on just this ground. In its conclusions it argued that ordained ministers are prohibited from being 'practising' homosexuals whereas, it argued, it may be acceptable in certain circumstances for lay people to live together in a homosexual partnership. It is stated with great subtlety and reserve: 'While unable, therefore, to commend the way of life just described as in itself as faithful a reflection of God's purposes in creation as the heterophile, we do not reject those who sincerely believe it is God's call to them.'[15]

Despite the subtlety of the argument, this was seen by some as both a failure to 'guard the tradition' and a failure to interpret with integrity what they saw as the unequivocal condemnation of homosexual practices by the scriptural witness. Others were scandalised by the report for almost precisely the opposite reasons. They believed that there were inherent contradictions in the argument. If lay people are allowed to live within homosexual partnerships, how could ministers be refused such a lifestyle? Is it not the case that a dynamic view of Scripture, within the context of tradition and the life of the Church, allows for the development of new teaching for a new culture? This is not the place to comment on the adequacy of the report and its arguments. It is clear, however, that precisely the issues that we have raised are crystallised in the report. It is not disingenuous to applaud the bishops for identifying with honesty and courage the very crux of the use of Scripture within reflections on authority in the Church.

Effectively, Scripture raises many of the issues which need to be explored more widely in relation to authority in the Church. Anglicanism has never pursued a pattern of authority that is *sola scriptura*. This Reformation doctrine, which attempted to root all authority within the Church in holy Scripture, was not embraced by the early Anglican apologists. Both the Thirty-Nine Articles and later declarations of faith have implied instead the sufficiency of Scripture. Such a position immediately requires interpretation and implies the possibility of development. The tradition is dynamic and thus so is the Church's authority.

The quotation from David Lodge early on in this chapter caricatured what he implied are facile and dogmatic attitudes held by the Church. The Church is approached with the eyes of fundamentalism. There is a literal approach to its teaching and an assumption of absolute authority. An equally good case can be made for caricaturing certain attitudes to the Bible and its use to support the authority structures of the Church. Where the Bible is understood literally, where the different genres within the Old and New Testaments are treated as in exact parallel to each other, then an inadequate hermeneutic will result. Similarly, if the Bible is used as a manual from which one may read off ready-made answers to the various social, moral and political questions of the day, then a simplistic understanding will result. This will lead to inevitable and parallel consequences for authority in the Church, if the Bible is used to underpin a static model of the tradition and authority. The bishops within synod have the unenviable task of discernment that makes them guardians of a dynamic tradition. The inductive approach to authority which is essential to Anglican polity lends itself to this dynamic process, which still honours the place of a continuing tradition. It was Edmund Burke who argued that institutions must be open to reform but that these same institutions are summarily abolished at our peril. A healthy attitude to the place of Scripture in the continued renewal of authority patterns will pay careful heed to Burke's warning.

◉ 9 ◉

Authority and the Chair of Augustine

Presiding from a chair

Norwich Cathedral is the only cathedral in Northern Europe where the ancient bishop's throne has retained its place 'high and lifted up' at the east end of the cathedral. Placed in the apsidal east end of the presbytery, this was the position favoured in Romanesque cathedrals universally all the way through to the twelfth century. It reflected the primitive Byzantine pattern which was itself imperial and secular in origin. In the Aula Palatina, in the Roman city of Trier, we see a secular basilica again with an apsidal east end. The governor would have sat at the centre of the apse flanked by his advisers. The Christian church adopted this pattern. It is seen classically in the basilican church of Santa Sabina on the Aventine Hill in Rome. Within a Christian basilica, the bishop would have sat at the centre of the apse flanked by either the cathedral chapter or by other priests of the diocese who acted as his senior advisers.

When, in July 1977, the Chair of Augustine in Canterbury Cathedral was moved back from the eastern Corona chapel to its present position behind the high altar, this was a reversion to the Byzantine practice which we have just described. This thirteenth-century stone chair or throne may well have been a copy of the earlier cathedra used by the first archbishops. It represents the continuity of the see of Canterbury and the focus of the authority of the archbishop. The recovery of this ancient position for the chair was far more than a matter of aesthetics. Symbolically, it reinforces the focal role of the archbishop not only in the diocese of Canterbury but more widely within the Church of England. In Augustine's day the Church in England was only embryonic and jurisdiction purely local. Even by the time of Anselm (archbishop from 1093 to 1114) the archbishop of Canterbury's universal jurisdiction within England was still a matter of controversy. By the later Middle Ages, however, Canterbury's primacy in England was established and the Chair of Augustine took on a greater significance.

The growth of the worldwide Anglican Communion gives to the chair a still greater pre-eminence, for the archbishop of Canterbury now enjoys a primacy of honour throughout all the Anglican provinces. As we have seen, the office of archbishop of Canterbury is effectively one of the 'instruments' whereby communion is maintained. Symbolically, this has been further emphasised by another more recent development in Canterbury Cathedral. At the time of the 1988 Lambeth Conference the 'compass rose' (a symbol of the Anglican Communion) was set into the floor of the cathedral at the eastern end of the nave. The cathedral has thus taken on a stronger sense of being the 'mother church' of the communion.

There are other moves which have increased this sense of leadership of the archbishop of Canterbury within the communion. Since the early 1980s there has been, at Lambeth Palace, a Secretary for Anglican Communion Affairs who is a full member of the archbishop's personal staff. Furthermore, successive archbishops have used one of the 'provincial canonries' within the General Chapter of Canterbury Cathedral to honour the Secretary-General of the Anglican Communion. In other words, both structure and functions of staff have begun to reflect a developing role for the archbishop of Canterbury within the wider communion. The legacy of Augustine's mission, captured symbolically in the great chair behind Canterbury's high altar, has developed into a worldwide primacy of honour, but not of jurisdiction.

We have traced this development from the eighteenth century onwards with the growth of overseas bishoprics. The first Lambeth Conference of 1867 was a landmark in the growth of the influence of the see of Canterbury more widely. Archbishops Longley and Tait played seminal roles in this development, but from these early days of an emerging communion of autonomous provinces the arch-bishop's role has always been one of great sensitivity and subtlety. In his enthronement sermon, in March 1980, Robert Runcie cap-tured this eloquently. He commented on the expectations that some might have of an archbishop of Canterbury:

> Of course the Church has often tried to take short cuts to authority, enforcing respect and obedience by worldly means and so obscuring the face of God. I have inherited a substantial supply of weapons which once equipped the archbishop's private army. Men of power sat in that chair and their pikes now decorate the walls of Lambeth Palace.[1]

Later in that sermon the archbishop reflected upon his authority within the Anglican Communion, using the church in Africa as an example. He argued that the image of authority deriving from pikes and private armies is hardly appropriate:

> There is no place in our understanding of authority for the Archbishop of Canterbury to visit Africa like some reigning monarch descending on a viceroy. I shall be there to share what we have in England with our brothers and sisters and to learn what they have to teach us about personal discipline and sacrifice, and about the fresh joy of being a new follower of Christ.[2]

In retrospect, doubtless Robert Runcie would admit that in practice it was not quite like that. My memories of triumphal arches, woven from banana-leaf fronds, in a remote Bangladeshi village spoke more of a visiting potentate than of a simple brother. Even so, the archbishop's reflections on the paradoxes of being seen as an authority figure remain an accurate assessment of expectations and realities.

Perils of an Anglican papacy

In a penetrating but often off-beam article, Paul Vallely wrote:

> The Archbishop of Canterbury is starting to look like an Anglican pope.... Traditionally, church historians are fond of saying that an Archbishop of Canterbury has at least four jobs... it is in the last area [that as leader of the Anglican Communion] that papal comparisons arise.[3]

Vallely is right in saying that papal comparisons are often made and, as we shall see later, are even expected on some occasions from within the communion. The reality is, however, that from the first Lambeth Conference onwards no such jurisdiction was built into the archbishop of Canterbury's role. Indeed, archbishops did not wish to stake claims for such a place within Anglican authority structures. They did not desire to become popes. Experience has shown that the papal model itself is now open to criticism and is ripe for change. Vatican II implied a far more collegial pattern, and in the most recent encyclical on Christian unity the pope himself hinted at change. The pope reaffirmed the principle of collegiality but then developed a far-reaching reflection on the 'primacy of the see of Peter'. He wrote:

> When addressing the Ecumenical Patriarch His Holiness Dimitrios I, I acknowledged my awareness that for a great variety of reasons, and against the will of all concerned, what should have been a service sometimes manifested itself in a very different light.

The pope went on to ask: 'Could not the real but imperfect communion between us [there he is referring to all Churches] persuade Church leaders and their theologies to engage with me in a patient and fraternal dialogue on this subject [the primacy of the see of Peter]?'[4]

Roman Catholicism has frequently been criticised for overdeveloped patterns of primacy and hierarchical authority. The pope's reflections noted above suggest that there is at least the realisation that the present patterns of primacy and jurisdiction would be unacceptable and unworkable in a future united Christendom. In his article Paul Vallely is right to argue, as he does, that the authority of the archbishop of Canterbury is moral rather than juridical. It was for this reason that many commentators feared the fragmentation of the Anglican Communion following the 1988 Lambeth Conference. It seemed inconceivable, following the deep divisions over the issue of the ordination of women to the priesthood and the episcopate, that communion could be sustained. In the event it was sustained, and effectively so, through the archbishop of Canterbury's moral authority and the focusing of issues of communion and authority within Anglicanism upon the office of the archbishop. It is ultimately through that *office* and not the individual personality of the office-holder (as Vallely and others have argued) that communion is sustained. Some strengthening of that moral authority through a clearer definition of the archbishop of Canterbury's role as an 'instrument of communion' may be an essential part of clarifying patterns of authority in Anglicanism more widely.

Augustine's statesman?

History does not suggest that St Augustine of Canterbury was an internationalist or, indeed, a diplomat by instinct. On his journey from Rome Augustine suffered from a faint heart more than once. Bede reminds us that Pope Gregory the Great had to encourage and press Augustine forward in the mission to which he had been committed. At Autun, in Burgundy, Augustine was attracted both by the climate and the friendliness of the people; the prospect of preaching to the unfriendly and heathen English in a colder more northerly clime did not appeal to him. Bede recounts how, after arriving in England, Augustine met with the British (Welsh) bishops. The meeting was not propitious, not the least due to Augustine's lack of diplomacy.

Augustine's most recent successors have found themselves in a very different world. Because of the worldwide growth of Anglicanism, despite the distinctly non-papal model, archbishops of

Canterbury have to some extent had the mantle of international ecclesiastical statesman thrust upon them. A cluster of events in early 1990 focuses this point very clearly. In January 1990 Robert Runcie, then archbishop of Canterbury, paid an official visit to the patriarch of Ethiopia. It was an auspicious time for an international visit. Ethiopia remained locked in civil war, with the Marxist regime of President Mengistu engaged in bitter conflict with the Tigrean rebels. The country was also devastated by a very severe famine; indeed, this was one of the first occasions on which television pricked the conscience of the Western world with tragic pictures of millions of starving and diseased children. In the days immediately before the archbishop's visit Church and secular agencies were busy trying to broker a deal so that desperately needed food and medical supplies could be taken to the worst-hit areas. It was the arrival of the archbishop, as a neutral international figure, that finally allowed this deal to be concluded.

While the archbishop was in Ethiopia, the war in Nagorno-Karabakh (within Azerbaijan) flared up with a new intensity. There was much pressure from the Armenian community across the world for religious and political leaders to show support. Anglicans, and notably archbishops of Canterbury, had been supportive to the Armenian community for more than a century. In the late nineteenth century, Archbishop Benson had shown an interest in the Armenian Church and people, and during the Armenian genocide of 1916 Archbishop Randall Davidson had courageously intervened. There was pressure, then, on Archbishop Runcie to comment. Lambeth Palace contacted him in Ethiopia (he was actually extracted from a dinner given in his honour by the patriarch) to consult on making a statement. A carefully prepared communiqué was issued which took into account the complexity of the international issues. Azeri sensitivities were not ignored. The archbishop had to demonstrate that he had sophisticated and well-tuned political antennae.

If this was an episode that required the skills of diplomacy, the next incident – only two weeks later – demanded of the archbishop firmness and not a little courage. By now the archbishop was in

Dhaka, the capital of Bangladesh. As is generally the case he paid a courtesy call on the head of state, then President Ershad. Alongside the diplomatic pleasantries, the archbishop was able to raise the question of the plight of various political prisoners unjustly detained. Included among these prisoners were some Christians. This gave the archbishop the pretext for raising the issue. It also allowed the Church of Bangladesh bishop of Dhaka, Barnabas Mondal, to have his first-ever meeting with the state president. A few weeks later saw the release of the political detainees. These negotiations were not simple, since the archbishop's party was entirely dependent on the Bangladeshi Air Force for helicopter transport throughout the visit!

More recently, Archbishop George Carey has similarly used this aspect of his office to good effect. During his first visit to Israel after becoming primate, the archbishop met with the then prime minister, Yitzhak Shamir. In a friendly but frank exchange, Dr Carey was able to express his fears about the dwindling Christian community in Israel; he argued that that community might be strengthened and supported if different policies were pursued by the Israeli government in respect of the Palestinian population. Elsewhere, Dr Carey has also been able to assist in establishing relationships between the primates of provinces and their heads of state. In 1994, as archbishop he was able to facilitate a meeting between the prime minister and the primate of Canada; they had not yet previously met. In Malaysia in 1993, the archbishop was able to build some useful bridges between the prime minister and the bishop of West Malaysia.

On this level one of the most useful exchanges was between Archbishop Carey and President Moi in Kenya. In this case the Church had spoken out quite properly about human rights abuses in Kenya. This had caused the Church, and particularly the primate, Archbishop Manasses Kuria, to be very unpopular with the government. Archbishop Kuria asked the archbishop of Canterbury to mediate, which he did most effectively, and as a result the entire Kenyan House of Bishops was invited to meet with President Moi. This led at least to a temporary *rapprochement*. This has not only been the case in the archbishop's relationship with other Anglican provinces – on occasion it has also allowed for his intervention in countries with no significant Anglican presence. Thus, in a rather different scenario, Archbishop Carey was also able to apply pressure through diplomats in London to give support to the Russian government in resisting calls for a new law which would have restricted religious freedom. Pressure for such a law had originated in certain circles of the Russian Orthodox Church.

In all these cases it is probably reasonable to argue that the archbishop of Canterbury receives this high profile by virtue of his constitutional position in the United Kingdom and his place in the order of precedence, immediately after the monarch. Undoubtedly, it is this accident of history that has given the archbishop's *office* the pre-eminence that allows him access to heads of state, and effectively when abroad to be treated himself almost as a head of state. In the article to which we have referred already, Paul Vallely makes the point that the positions of the pope and the archbishop of Canterbury are radically different. The pope is a head of state, with embassies around the world. He is the head of a government run by a huge bureaucracy with a billion Catholics, nominally at least within its sway.[5] The contrast is fair, but it ignores the archbishop of Canterbury's constitutional position within the United Kingdom and described above.

It is this constitutional role that lends to the archbishop's office an enhanced authority. As with many aspects of Anglicanism, inductive and pragmatic reasoning is the point of origin for extended theological reflection. In other words, in this case a theology of primacy springs from the opportunities that are made available to the archbishop by virtue of his office. On some occasions, the archbishop's focal position offers ecclesiological opportunities too, well beyond the limits of the Anglican Communion. In Chile, for example, in 1991, Roman Catholic bishops had become increasingly concerned that they had had no contact with the leaders of the increasingly successful Pentecostal Churches; many members of these Churches had seceded from the Roman Catholic Church. Archbishop Runcie suggested that both sets of Church leaders should be invited to meet with him and a number of other clergy – Roman Catholics, Anglicans and a few Pentecostalists. This they agreed to do. It was the first such meeting ever and opened up the possibility of dialogue between the two communities of Christians. This constructive encounter was made possible both through the archbishop's high constitutional profile and also through what he described as the Anglican Church's 'ecumenical vocation'. In this case, as an episcopally ordered Church it could be respected by the Roman Catholic hierarchy, and as a Church born of the Reformation there could be constructive dialogue with the Pentecostal Churches.

Primus inter pares

It is in this area that there is perhaps the greatest gulf between theory and practice, expectations and reality. We have rehearsed fully, both in historical context and to some extent theologically, the archbishop of Canterbury's role within the Anglican Communion. While it is undoubtedly the case that the archbishop has no jurisdiction outside the Church of England, and also that the provinces assert their autonomy with vigour, nevertheless in practice his authority is increased by the demands and expectations placed upon him from different parts of the communion. In other words, despite all the qualifications, there appears to be a psychological and even practical need to have a clear, single figure of authority within the Anglican Communion.

This truth is manifested in different ways in different parts of the world. The Episcopal Church in the USA, for example, is fiercely independent. Its constitution is fashioned out of the need to declare itself a non-colonial Church; this was borne out in the earlier chapter on the history of the communion. In contrast to this, however, the archbishop of Canterbury is often lionised and frequently offered deference by American Anglicans. One could argue that this is simply one more demonstration of 'New World' warmth and immediacy. There is no doubt, however, that the honour given to the archbishop of Canterbury runs deeper than that. There is a real acceptance of his moral authority which rises above suspicions about a Lambeth curia or surreptitious influence from the Church of England.

In Africa the atmosphere is quite different. In the provinces of South and Central Africa there is a healthy respect which breathes an appropriate interdependence; the primacies of Desmond Tutu and Khotso Makhulu have nurtured this encouraging tendency. Elsewhere in Africa the feeling is often quite dissimilar. Part of this may issue from the fact that developing countries retain a complicated ambivalence towards what was seen as the 'mother country' and its Church. Thus, there is both a desire for independence yet also a deference to the see of Canterbury. Often there is despair in such provinces that the archbishop does not give a stronger lead, especially on contentious issues. Oddly enough, it may be the very autonomy that provinces say they cherish so much that has increased the focal position of the archbishop of Canterbury as *primus inter pares*. The stress on autonomy has weakened links between provinces and 'mother Churches', leaving a vacuum at the centre. As authority becomes increasingly dispersed, so the need increases to focus around some sort of 'centre', hence the increased moral authority of Augustine's successor. There are obvious dangers here if we are to take seriously both the collegiality and the significance of the lay voice which Anglicanism has said that it values. Admittedly, on occasion there are still rebellions within the councils of Anglicanism; at the 1993 meeting of the Anglican Consultative Council a member resigned in the belief that the agenda had been radically changed through the personal fiat of the archbishop of Canterbury.

The truth is that his lack of jurisdiction makes it difficult for the archbishop to intervene more widely within the communion unless he is asked to do so. Certainly the archbishop is, on occasion, asked to intervene in provincial disputes. Sometimes he will act as a counsellor or mediator himself, and on other occasions he will ask another primate to head a delegation to a divided province. French Chang Him, previously archbishop of the Indian Ocean, went to Rwanda at the height of the troubles there. Khotso Makhulu, the archbishop of Central Africa, was sent to try to unravel the impossible schism within the Episcopal Church of the Sudan. The Church again became united and the factions reconciled.

More *pares* than *primus*?

One of the dangers that should now be becoming apparent is the chasm which may easily develop between expectation and reality. Difficulties also arise due to the discrepancies between the authority given to the archbishop by virtue of his *office*, and the lack of any clear structure of authority within Anglicanism. In an unpublished paper from January 1988, Archbishop Runcie asked:

> What sort of Communion is it in which one Province ordains women to the priesthood – and soon, it might reasonably be expected, to the episcopate – whilst others are a long way from ordaining women to the diaconate? ... What sort of Communion is it where one Archbishop – the Archbishop of Sydney – consecrates bishops for the Church of England in South Africa (a church not in communion with Canterbury or the other Provinces of the Anglican Communion) without the permission or approval of the Anglican Province there?

He went on to argue that it is a particularly bad time for the chairman of the House of Bishops of the Church of England to attempt to begin to exercise a more disciplinary role in international Anglicanism. One alternative to this would, of course, be to elect a bishop from another province from within the communion to the see of Canterbury. Putting to one side for a moment the issues posed here for Establishment, such a move would either imply a papal model of the sort we have already rejected, or it would perhaps decrease the sense of *primus inter pares* still further. The authority which we have seen deriving from the archbishop's constitutional position in Britain would disappear, and he would easily be captured by what might become increasingly power-hungry structures of international ecclesiastical bureaucracy.

One of the problems is setting the archbishop of Canterbury's role clearly within the other structures of Anglicanism without letting him be captured by them. It is by virtue of his constitutional role in the United Kingdom that he is often accorded honour more widely within Anglicanism It is presumably also because of those same historical accidents that it has been deemed unnecessary for so long to place the role of the archbishop within a more structured context within the Anglican Communion. This has not only been true in international structures. There has been a lack of clarity, for example, since the inception of synodical government in the Church of England about the real meaning of the authority of the 'bishop in synod'. This lack is mirrored within the international structures of Anglicanism. The Anglican Consultative Council is precisely what it claims to be, a consultative body. It has no jurisdiction or canonical power. The Lambeth Conference, similarly, is consultative, albeit with a greater moral authority and a clear structural linkage with provincial Houses of Bishops. The Primates' Meeting may be the place from which to begin a more structured pattern for the maintenance of communion within Anglicanism. It may also be the organ within which initially to set the archbishop's primacy of honour. It may be the body from which we can begin to model a clear pattern of collegiality.

Gathering around a chair?

We began this chapter with the bishop's throne in Norwich Cathedral. Even though it is set high up at the east end of the cathedral, its position within the apse avoids an undue sense of the bishop ruling over his people. Instead, with his chapter flanking him, and the wide presbytery before him, it suggests a pattern of the people of God, with their shepherd gathering around the altar of God to celebrate the sacrament of the Eucharist, the sacrament of the coming kingdom. Robert Runcie has often talked of the archbishop of Canterbury 'gathering but not ruling' the Anglican Communion. This has continued to be the model in practice. Although Archbishop George Carey has travelled more than any of his predecessors as archbishop of Canterbury, and despite this increasing concentration on the wider Anglican Communion, he has continued to exercise a primacy of care and support rather than a primacy of rule. Indeed, some have even argued that the archbishop of Canterbury's leadership is modelled on a pattern where authority is deliberately given away. By this means, paradoxically, he is better able to influence those who share that authority with him. It is an extension of the notion of dispersed authority. It resonates well with the incarnational rhythms of Christianity. God has sometimes been described by Christian theologians as 'the God who gives himself away'.

As we have seen, however, so many of the pressures upon an archbishop of Canterbury in the contemporary world, for very different reasons, drive the dynamics of the structures in precisely the opposite direction. There is an almost irresistible urge to focus power and authority on one individual office rather than to allow that office to exercise an appropriate authority collegially with fellow primates and bishops and ultimately with the whole people of God. Here the pressures derive from a lack of clarity in the international structures, their interrelationship with each other and the role and function expected of each part of the structure, that is, each instrument of communion. The need to take account of these forces is all the more important since the office of the archbishop of Canterbury is itself a 'developing institution'.

Within the Church of England the precise nature of the office has developed for a variety of different reasons. First of all, the notion of 'Establishment' has broadened. Although the Church of England remains 'by law established', the model of Establishment has changed. The archbishop is often now seen as the protector of people 'of any religion or none'. Muslims and Jews in Britain are in no hurry to dismantle Establishment, since it keeps a religious focus at the heart of the nation's life, not least within parliament. Secondly, the establishment of synodical government has sharpened the archbishop of Canterbury's role within the Church of England through his ex-officio chairing of the House of Bishops. There are increasing pressures towards a more centralised and less 'diocesan' Church. At the time of writing consideration is being given by various organs within the Church of England to the report of the Archbishops'

Commission on the Organisation of the Church of England. If this were accepted in anything like the form proposed, then an 'Archbishops' Council' would be established, chaired by the archbishop of Canterbury. This would be responsible for focusing policy and expediting decisions. At present it is too early to say precisely how the Church of England will respond to these proposals. Whatever response is made, however, it will affect the archbishop of Canterbury's role only in relation to the Church of England. Furthermore, its ecclesiological implications are likely to be minimal.[6]

Finally, the media, which effectively acts as the interpreter of modern society, has placed increasing expectations upon the archbishop who it rightly perceives to be a national figure. He is conceived of by the press in quasi-prime ministerial terms. The press relishes question time at the General Synod; it is a moment when the archbishop can be pushed back against the ropes of the ecclesiastical boxing ring. Increasingly, the archbishop is seen as the mouthpiece of the Church of England.

Many of these developments are unavoidable and, given careful reflection with an eye to the structures, may even become positive developments. That they may become so, however, requires us to be reflective and protective of the institutions of the Anglican Church, including the office of the archbishop of Canterbury. Edmund Burke, to whom we referred earlier, spoke of the danger of overthrowing institutions. Instead, he argued for their reasoned development. Precisely the same can be argued for in relation to the office of the archbishop of Canterbury, not only within the Church of England but within worldwide Anglicanism. Such an approach requires the Church to reflect upon all its structures and to see how the role of the archbishop fits into this wider context. Changes within society nationally and internationally make changes within the authority structures of the Church and the role of the archbishop inevitable. The archbishop of Canterbury is, in Burkian terms, a developing institution. What is not inevitable, however, is the precise pattern of structures, the precise model of authority. Some of the parameters are clearly within the hands of the Church. We are not driven inexorably either to an Anglican pseudo-papal structure or to a position where authority is so dispersed as to lead the communion into anarchy.

Two pictures come to mind at this point. They refer, as it happens, to two different archbishops, but their vividness relates to the *office* and not to the personalities. When the Anglican Consultative Council met in Cardiff in 1990, we were treated to three weeks of scorching weather. On a number of occasions Archbishop Runcie could be seen sheltering under a modest tree, receiving an endless stream of people consulting him and asking advice. Sitting there rather like an Anglican guru, after the model of Jesus beneath the fig tree in the first chapter of John's gospel, the archbishop's structural relationship to the conference was marginal. He is its president, but rarely needs to preside. The meeting itself has no power directly to change things within worldwide Anglicanism, and yet the archbishop's presence was still an essential if eccentric ingredient. The stream of people consulting with him presses this point home. The second picture is of Archbishop Carey at Cumberland Lodge, in Windsor Great Park, chairing the Primates' Meeting in 1995. He had gathered around him the primates from the four corners of the earth, and with patient but clear chairmanship he helped focus the mind of the meeting. Here the archbishop of Canterbury is clearly the chairman of a meeting of bishops who themselves have a primacy in their own provinces. This meeting, however, again has no clear or essential structural interaction with the Anglican Consultative Council. The two run in parallel. Ultimately, then, both these pictures include essential and different facets of the archbishop of Canterbury's role, but these facets must be brought together within clearer structures if Anglicanism is to offer a useful model of authority to the wider Church.

Perhaps the key lies in the Primates' Meeting. How can the archbishop of Canterbury be supported effectively to be the 'first among equals'? How can he help the primates develop a real collegiality within the process of decision-making? Beginning with those questions, one can begin to explore the relationship of the Primates' Meeting to the Lambeth Conference, the synods of each of the provinces, and the Anglican Consultative Council. This may assist Anglicans in pioneering a true collegiality which includes the lay voice and which does not fudge the issue of 'bishop in synod', nor opt for a model which simply apes secular models of democratic government. How can this move us on towards a more Benedictine model of the 'abbot in chapter', where the abbot's role is to discern consensus and identify clearly the process of reception? Such a model clearly sees the archbishop of Canterbury gathering and not ruling. The Chair of Augustine gathers the worldwide Anglican Communion around the common table of the sacrament of the coming kingdom.

❦ 10 ❧

Authority and the World

In but not *of* the world

For some there can be no more potent symbol of ecclesiastical authority than that of Thomas à Becket in his tragic struggle with King Henry II of England. In happier times a close counsellor of the king, on becoming archbishop of Canterbury Becket found himself fairly soon locked in mortal combat with the monarch. There are many ironies relating to the story. As with many whom the Church has canonised, Becket's sanctity was a two-edged sword. In defending the Church against the incursions of the State, he was protecting clerical privileges in a manner that we might now find it hard to defend. Nevertheless, Becket's stand against the king, and his martyrdom, point up for us another key aspect of the Church's authority. The martyrdom of Becket reminds us that the Church is set in the world to live out the prophetic ministry of Christ, and through that ministry to proclaim the Gospel of God. Much of what we have discussed thus far relates to the internal ordering of the Church, its doctrines and its structures for decision-making. Authority in the Church also has immediate and direct implications for the world in which the Church is set. This should affect the mode in which authority patterns are set up and exercised within the Church. They should be an example and not a scandal to the world.

In his enthronement sermon at Canterbury, with a memorable image Robert Runcie reflected:

149

You know how sometimes in an English garden you will find a maze. The trouble is to get to the centre of all those hedges. It is easy to get lost. I had a dream of a maze. There were some people very close to the centre. . . . But just outside the gate others were standing. They were further from the heart of the maze. . . . I long to be able to speak, while archbishop, with men and women who stand outside the Christian Church. I would say to them, 'You can teach us much if together we could look for the secret of the maze-like muddle in which the world finds itself.'[1]

The attitudes implied here lie close to the heart of Anglicanism. The authority patterns described earlier, where Church and world are inextricably caught up into each other, implies an openness of weave. It is such an openness to culture that has encouraged a healthy attitude to scholarship in Anglicanism which supports a critical approach. It is similar values which lend to Anglican moral teaching a tendency to incorporate rather than to exclude contextual and pastoral considerations. An allowance for the contingencies of nature and history derives to some extent from the English empiricism within which the beginnings of Anglican scholarship flourished and grew. This aversion to absolutism offers to Anglican polity a means of communicating the truths of Christian teaching to wider society in a manner which challenges the world. It does so without being exclusive or by using an introverted dogmatism.

If this is to remain the case, then, Anglicans must continually reflect upon their models of authority. The mode in which that authority is exercised should be exemplary for the wider world, but patterns of consultation and attempts to focus, wherever possible, a consensus within the Church should remain primary to this task. The model pioneered by St Benedict where the 'abbot in chapter' helps to achieve this is the most persuasive model, as we shall see in our concluding chapter. There is a sense in which the Church must be prepared to 'earn its own' authority, if it is to be taken seriously by wider society. Given that it is capable of earning such respect, the Christian Church can then expect to be understood as 'an authority' to be taken seriously within wider society. It will contribute, alongside other agencies and organs within society, to the formulation of social policy and a common core of moral truths.

It would be naïve to suggest that the focusing of consensus in these matters will be easily achieved or, indeed, without conflict. Such would certainly not have been the case, for example, with Benedict and his disciples. There is often a naïvety abroad in relation to religious communities; the human condition with its conflicts and uncertainties is experienced just as dramatically there as within natural families and wider society. Benedict's rule cannot, of course, be simply translated to problems of authority in all circumstances. Different patterns exist, and it is necessary to relate to myriad conditions within the variety of cultures across the world. The Church (and not just Anglicanism) has had to adapt to the varied conditions prevailing in a great array of different cultures. In some cases this has called for prophecy and in others for support of a faltering democracy.

This complex series of patterns within different societies was analysed classically by Richard Niebuhr in his review of Christianity and culture,[2] in which he sets out a variety of different models. What we might loosely describe as the 'prophetic model', Niebuhr labelled *Christ against culture*. A liberal accommodation to society he calls *the Christ of culture*. Other patterns are also described. These embrace dualism, a synthesis of Christianity and culture, and finally a model rooted in redemption where Christ is the *transformer of culture*. Niebuhr does not insist that any one of these models is mandatory, although it is the redemptive model, where Christ transforms culture, that is the culmination of his argument. Even so, he writes: 'Yet it must be evident that neither extension nor refinement of study could bring us to the conclusive result that would enable us to say, "This is the Christian answer."'[3]

Niebuhr's ultimate conclusion is that believers, and the Church itself, must ground themselves in a faith which is eschatological, that is, a faith which looks to a future remade in God. Since we have not yet arrived at that 'end time', and as we continue to live our lives in the world, the precise model which the Church chooses to engage with society will necessarily relate to the relativities and contingencies of each unique situation. This has been clearly illustrated in the experience of Anglicanism through the great variety of cultures within which it now thrives. In each case the response has been different.

Critical solidarity

Anglicanism, so to speak, 'cut its teeth' on the relationship between Church and State in England. It was this that allowed it to develop its own *modus vivendi* which sought for an effective way of expressing Christian moral authority within society. This cannot be seen as the pattern for all Anglican provinces. Indeed, the Church of England is unique in being the only province within the Anglican Communion where the Church is still Established. Even so, it may be that some of the attitudes which are often seen as typical of Anglicanism in this realm of moral authority found their earliest fashioning within the Church of England. Church and State live alongside each other, and there is a healthy mutual influence and critique.

In recent years within Britain this process of engagement has developed further. During the 1980s the archbishop of Canterbury became good press copy. The media enjoyed constructing powerful contrasts between the politics of the government of Margaret Thatcher and the social ethical teaching of the Church of England. The Falklands War memorial service at St Paul's Cathedral in London and the *Faith in the City* report on 'urban priority areas' were but two cases in point. Church and State were depicted as being at loggerheads. Interest from the press in the Church and social comment has by no means abated, and the present archbishop of Canterbury, Dr George Carey, has found himself at the centre of similar controversies, government policy on prisons being just one example.

Both Archbishops Runcie and Carey have continued to work within the broad establishment of the Church of England, but they have not allowed these traditional structures to blunt their criticism of social policy where they feel this to have been necessary. The model which has developed has been labelled one of 'critical solidarity'. As part of the Establishment, the Church cannot pretend to a prophetic separation that does not exist. The Church of England is to a large extent dependent upon the structures of the Establishment for its own platform, and the presence of bishops in the House of Lords presses this point home. At the same time, this does not require of the Church an unerring support for each successive government in all of its policies, hence the label 'critical solidarity'.

The background to this position was set out well in a classical analysis of the Church of England's relationship to the political order by Giles Ecclestone, who wrote: 'The Church is both part of the world, and called into being as an instrument of God's mission to the world. This is the dual reality with which we must live.'[4] Later on he reflects:

> The Church ... can fossilise. A socially responsible Church can forget that it is part of the society it is seeking to change. In various subtle ways it may by its institutional life and attitudes be perpetuating features of social life which it is formally committed to changing. It needs to find ways in which it can be addressed by its critics and see through their eyes.[5]

This philosophy lies at the heart of 'critical solidarity', which in itself is the essence of the approach taken by recent archbishops of Canterbury and by the leadership of the Church of England as a whole. The so-called 'privatisation of morality' is one area in which Dr Carey has vociferously and consistently criticised contemporary society and (as the press would argue), by implication, the government. The privatisation of morality describes a cluster of attitudes which regard morality purely as a matter of private concern, instead of something which is held in trust by society for the common good. Morality becomes a matter of individual opinion rooted in no common core of ethical teaching. There is no sense in which morality is seen as being discovered, as an objective element within human existence. Instead, it is subjective and invented by each individual. Dr Carey has warned of the dangers and shortcomings of such an approach in a number of his public utterances. In one of his earliest interventions on this issue he argued:

> The privatisation of morality has radically dangerous consequences at different levels. The individual, who has the potential to reflect the goodness of God or the depths of evil, is vulnerable to unbridled selfishness and to a sense of futility and bewilderment if there is no absolute good and no absolute purpose to life. I sense that millions of our fellow citizens are struggling with the resulting spiritual emptiness.[6]

In perhaps his most high-profile public intervention in the realm of morals Dr Carey introduced a debate in the House of Lords in July 1996, highlighting the danger of allowing society to slip away from a common core of moral teaching. He cited the Chief Rabbi, Dr Jonathan Sacks, among others, in his support. At one point the archbishop argued:

> Moreover, we all know that the toughest moral decisions are not always between right and wrong, but between two 'rights' which pull in different directions. So we desperately need our young people to learn both the basic rules and the judgement needed with which to confront the constant dilemmas of life. This brings me to a partnership we need to secure between all involved in the important task of nurturing and forming young people today.[7]

It is this sense of partnership, seen on an even wider spectrum than the nurture of the young, that stands at the centre of 'critical solidarity'. It is this that has allowed the Church of England and (through a contemporary widening of ecclesiastical establishment) other British Churches to contribute towards the formulation of social policy and the framing of legislation. It is by this means that Christian authority has continued to play a significant part in the fashioning of contemporary society. When the Warnock Commission was set up to report on 'Human Fertilisation and Embryology' there were included on the commission both an Anglican professor of moral theology and also an Anglican lay woman with a background in counselling. It was that report that eventually helped the government in the framing of legislation, and also in setting up the statutory bodies which now oversee continuing work and research in this area.

In the 1960s, it was the Church of England report *Putting Asunder* which set out the principles which dictated the ethos of the 1969 Divorce Reform Act. Many would argue now that it was those elements which were excluded from the Act, but included in the Church report, that would have balanced the final legislation and avoided some of the later abuses. Much more recently, a joint submission from bishops in both the Church of England and the Roman Catholic Church in England and Wales has contributed to a House of Lords committee reporting on the ethics of euthanasia. The 1985 report *Faith in the City* was important in its effects upon the political debate on social policy.

All these contributions have been proactive, and invited by the government, though other significant interventions have been made reactively over the years. It was largely pressure from the Churches that caused the first Sunday Trading Bill to fall in parliament. Similarly, much pressure has been applied by the Churches on both Immigration and Asylum Bills. Revision and amendment to proposed legislation has often been made in the light of intervention by the Churches, and frequently this has been effected either directly through the archbishop of Canterbury or through contributions in debate made by the bishops in the House of Lords.

The foundations upon which such contributions are made are those of Christian moral reflection, and are often in the form of general principles rather than in the specifics of legislation. Archbishop William Temple coined the phrase 'middle axioms' for such general principles. Middle axioms stand midway between the broadest, most general moral principles and specific rules, laws and regulations within society. The application of such axioms allows the Christian moralist to apply reasonable pressure within society without going beyond his brief and being caught up in technical controversies which extend beyond his own competence. A widespread application of this theory is sometimes questioned, since it is easy for such axioms to slide in either direction; they either become too specific or too general. The process, however, has much to commend it. The Church can raise broad moral questions without entering directly into party politics. Dr Carey's interventions on the dangers of a privatised morality are a good example.

Prophetic authority

In certain situations and cultures those patterns described by the term 'critical solidarity' are inapplicable or inappropriate. They are less easily applied, for example, where the Church is not Established. They are insufficiently challenging where there is clear and blatant injustice. In such situations that approach which Richard Niebuhr describes as *Christ against culture* may be brought to bear. Perhaps the classical example of such a challenge was Desmond Tutu's resistance to both the principle and the practice of apartheid in South Africa. As secretary of the South African Council of Churches, and then successively as bishop of Johannesburg and archbishop of Cape Town, Desmond Tutu was fearless in his condemnation of apartheid and racism, and at times his freedom and privacy suffered because of this. Tutu stood in a long line of Anglican leaders who had opposed apartheid: both Gonville ffrench-Beytagh, when dean of Johannesburg, and Joost de Blank, when archbishop of Cape Town, were expelled from South Africa because of the line they took.

Tutu was supported in his stand by the 1988 Lambeth Conference when specific resolutions were tabled and passed in an attempt to apply further international pressure within the political process. A principled affirmation of Christian attitudes was set out in Resolution 39, which stated unequivocally: 'This Conference reaffirms its belief that the system of apartheid in South Africa is evil and especially repugnant because of the cruel way a tyrannical racist system is being upheld in the name of the Christian faith.'[8]

This last phrase is particularly telling, indicating as it does that Christian theology and tradition cannot be used to support racist policies. In many ways, the prophetic determination of this 1988 resolution was a great advance on the first and less specific resolution of the 1978 conference; this in a fairly general manner simply deplored all injustice and economic inequalities. The 1988 resolution spelt out practical ways in which Churches could aim to put pressure upon the South African government to bring about change. It is almost certain that when change did come, under the government of President F.W. de Klerk, the Churches were partially instrumental in bringing forward this change. Here was a clear case where the Churches (and particularly the Anglican Church in the Republic of South Africa) have earned the moral authority to speak about issues on behalf of wider society.

The Anglican Church in the Middle East has also taken a prophetic stance with regard to the injustices which have existed over the years in Israel and the 'Occupied Territories'. Here, an increasingly indigenous leadership has pressed the government of Israel over injustices within the Palestinian community. Bishop Samir Kafity, himself a Palestinian, has been courageously outspoken, not only on injustice but also on the dangerous levels of emigration from Israel within the dwindling Christian community. The Middle East is also a good example of where other provinces within the Anglican Communion have shown solidarity with this prophetic stance. Successive archbishops of Canterbury have shown support. Moreover, the presiding bishop of the Episcopal Church in the USA, Ed Browning, has shown a fearless determination to support Palestinian Christians and, indeed, the Palestinian community more generally.

Other examples of primates and senior bishops having a close and influential role in government, in a pastoral/prophetic way, can be cited. The late Archbishop George Browne in Liberia, Philip Mokuku in Lesotho, Dinis Sengulane in Mozambique, Stephen Mumba in Zambia and James Kauluma in Namibia have all had a creative role as their countries have moved through periods of political upheaval; often they have been significant in broking peace, sometimes sharing the role with Roman Catholic bishops. It may be that some of this has been reflective of the model of Anglicanism offered in earlier centuries by the Church of England as a national Church, and as part of the Reformation heritage.

Each of these examples highlights occasions or situations where Anglicans have believed that the Gospel requires them to challenge the *status quo* within a particular society. The scriptural witness as mediated within the tradition is applied to a contemporary issue. Often the issue is debated within the councils and synods of the Church, alongside direct interventions from bishops. Christian patterns of authority are seen to extend well beyond the bounds of the worshipping community itself to challenge injustice within society.

Reconciling authority

There is a further manifestation of this same authority being applied more widely in society which may at first sight appear to be identical with these prophetic interventions we have described. This is in cases where there is almost endemic division within society, sometimes rooted in splits within the Christian community itself and sometimes even colluded with by the Church. A clear instance of this was the case of the civil war in Rwanda in 1994, where both the Roman Catholic and Anglican Churches colluded with the violence which led eventually to genocide. Anglicanism worldwide condemned most vigorously the Church's collusion within these tragic events, and the archbishop of Canterbury intervened directly in the Anglican Church there in an attempt to arrest this collusion. Due to wider political pressures and the complexity of the situation in Rwanda it is difficult to assess the precise effects of the archbishop's intervention. What is clear, however, is that the crucial need in Rwanda is for reconciliation and not only prophecy.

The other most obvious example of the need for reconciliation within a community has been in Northern Ireland. The situation there is far too complex to analyse within these pages. Suffice to say that while some of the roots of the conflict are undoubtedly religious in the profound divisions between the Roman Catholic and Protestant communities, these have been exploited by politicians on both sides of the fence. The situation is made more complex and less accessible for effective Anglican intervention, since the chief antagonists are generally members either of the Roman Catholic Church or of various forms of Presbyterianism and not of the Church of Ireland. That is not to deny that Anglicans have been culpable in colluding with both prejudice and violence. It is simply to argue that there has been far less potential for effective intervention from Anglicans in the province of Northern Ireland.

Archbishop Robin Eames has worked tirelessly, however, to bring the two communities together, and built up a strong and trusting relationship with Cardinal Cahal Daly in attempts to break the deadlock between the two communities. Both Church leaders have been courageous, not only in their condemnation of violence, but also in attempting to use the influence of the Christian Church within the political process. Again, the 1988 Lambeth Conference expressed its support for both the Church of Ireland and Archbishop Eames in their efforts toward peace. Resolution 73 noted these key points:

This Conference:

(1) Expresses solidarity with fellow Anglicans and with all the people of Northern Ireland in their suffering.
(2) In the circumstances of Northern Ireland condemns all violence.
(3) Urges all political and community leaders to seize every opportunity to work together, to bring about a just and peaceful solution.[9]

The situation in both Rwanda and Northern Ireland is different from those described earlier inasmuch as reconciliation is perhaps the primary need, even though challenge and prophecy are often called for too. In Richard Niebuhr's analysis this comes closest to his notion of *Christ as the transformer of culture*, the product of what Niebuhr describes as a 'conversionist' mentality. The emphasis is clearly upon the motif of redemption within Christian theology. Niebuhr describes the conversionists' attitude at one point thus:

This is what human culture could be – a transformed human life in and to the glory of God. For man it is impossible, but all things are possible to God, who has created man, body and soul, for Himself, and sent his Son into the world that the world through him might be saved.[10]

It is in situations of this nature where the Church most clearly must earn its right to offer the insights of the Christian Gospel to wider society. Collusion with injustice and violence undermine the Church's own moral authority.

Authority expressed through communion

Through all the period under review the Anglican Communion in its consultative bodies, networks and studies has sought to fulfil the prophetic role in face of the profound social issues of our time, not only by condemning injustice but by proclaiming in hope the vision of God's kingdom and of a transformed humanity.[11]

Certainly that is true of the most recent history of the communion, as is clear from earlier references to the 1988 Lambeth Conference. It was not so obviously true, however, in earlier pan-Anglican consultations. It was the 1920 Lambeth Conference that most obviously broke through this barrier both in its resolutions on 'Social and Industrial Questions' and in its first section on 'Christianity and International Relations'. The human disaster represented by the First World War irreversibly altered perceptions of human progress – one poet characterised this in a famous line reflecting on the effects of the bitter conflict. His verdict was: 'Never such innocence again.' It was this challenging impact of the war that transformed Reinhold Niebuhr's liberalism into neo-orthodoxy and also awakened in Karl Barth similar theological emphases. There was a new awareness of humankind's fallenness and its need for redemption. The 1920 Lambeth Conference resolutions reflect these same concerns:

We rejoice that in these times of peril God is giving to his Church a fresh vision of purpose to establish a Kingdom in

which all the nations of the earth shall be united as one family
in righteousness and peace. We hold that this can only come
through an acceptance of the sovereignty of our Lord Jesus
Christ and of his teaching, and through the application of
the principles of brotherhood, justice and unselfishness, to
individuals and nations alike.[12]

The theological response to this new realism about humanity has
varied within Anglicanism in the years that have followed. Sometimes the response has been conservative and influenced by neo-
orthodoxy, whereas on other occasions there has been a liberal
challenge to the injustice of the *status quo*. Since 1920, however,
each Lambeth Conference has used its consultative authority to pass
resolutions relating to social justice. In 1930, 'Race' and 'Peace and
War' stood alongside a longer section on the moral questions relating
to 'Marriage and Sex'. In 1948, in the section 'The Church and the
Modern World', the resolutions addressed issues including 'Human
Rights', 'The Church and War', 'Palestine', 'The Church and the
Modern State', 'Communism and Education'. The 1958 conference
had a section on 'The Reconciling of Conflicts Between and Within
Nations'. Finally, the 1968 conference had scattered throughout its
deliberations resolutions on 'Man's Stewardship of Nature', 'Conser-
vation of the Seabed', 'War' and 'Human Unity'. The preoccupations
of the 1978 and 1988 conferences have already been mentioned.

This rapid overview of the past seven Lambeth Conferences is
not aimed to prove a comprehensive coverage of political, social and
moral issues starting from the standpoint of Christian authority, nor
is it intended to argue that the *process* adopted by Lambeth Conferences is an appropriate or effective means of influencing
governments and societies. Indeed, the passing of resolutions, often
without adequate debate, is one of the main criticisms of the pro-
cedure of Lambeth Conferences. Furthermore, on the wider canvas,
it is not immediately obvious that the issuing of statements is the
most effective way of influencing public policy. The point of this
brief survey is instead to illustrate how, as a communion, Anglicanism has increasingly begun to appreciate the significance of issues

of authority in relation to social and moral questions. This indicates on this level a developing sense of solidarity as a communion, together with a responsibility to the wider world.

In a frequently quoted aphorism, Archbishop William Temple noted how 'the Church is the only institution which exists for those outside itself'. This is an essential reflection to remember whenever we discuss authority within the Church. It is easy for the Church, like any other institution, to become introverted and 'navel-gazing'. Issues which relate to its own structure, liturgy and doctrine easily allow discussion to tend in this direction. The issue of authority, however, must be seen in the widest context of the mission of the Church, the ministry of Christ and the proclamation of the Gospel. If the Church is concerned with its own structures and patterns of authority, it is only so interested for three reasons.

First of all, the Church is charged with guarding and handing over the truth of the Gospel to each successive generation. Patterns of authority are essential if it is to achieve this; traditionally, this is part of the role of the episcopate. In speaking of the Church, the distinction is often made of mission and maintenance; the first is abhorred, the second is lauded. This contrast fails to take seriously that each needs the other. Without the maintenance of congregations, buildings, worship and authority there will be no structure from which to facilitate mission. Equally, without a clear commitment to wider society, mission will die and all structures of the Church become obsolete and, indeed, redundant. Authority must be for the world.

Second, the Church is charged with proclaiming that truth afresh to each generation. The context in which the Gospel is proclaimed is constantly changing. This does not argue for a thorough-going relativism, but it does require the Church to take seriously the relativities presented by a fast-changing society. This has implications both for the way in which Christian doctrine is articulated and also for the effective expression of the ethical imperatives of the Gospel within the secular world. The truth of the Gospel includes clear teaching, for example, on justice and social stability within society. Authority within the Church again has direct relevance here.

Finally, the manner in which the Church exercises authority ought to be exemplary. It should be a pattern that it would be happy to see followed within all human institutions. This directs us back to the New Testament and to the mission of Jesus. The pattern of Jesus's life and death is distinctive. His encounter with the secular authorities during his passion is one of great subtlety in all the gospel accounts. Authority is exercised without force or oppression.

If these three principles are essential, then authority within the Church must be for the world and not just for the Church. How can Anglicans within individual parishes and churches, within provinces and throughout the communion, effectively exercise such authority within our contemporary world? Will there be resonances with the authority given by Pope Gregory the Great when he first sent Augustine from Rome to bring the Gospel to the Angles?

✎ 11 ✑

A Future Pattern of Authority

What, then, are the issues?

At the end of the first chapter of this book two or three general
questions set the scene for the discussion that has followed. Perhaps
the two key questions raised were: What is an appropriate attitude
to authority within the Christian Church at the present time? What
can Anglican thought and practice contribute to such attitudes and
to the development of a clear but nuanced Christian exercise of
authority? The later chapters have attempted to answer these questions in respect of a communion which has developed into a
worldwide body over the past 200 and more particularly past 100
years. We shall not rehearse those arguments again in summary, but
instead we shall look more specifically at the implications for the
Anglican Church worldwide and its present instruments of communion. Before we move on to do that, some preliminary scene-
setting is necessary.

First of all, it has become clear that authority implies 'reasoned
acceptance'. The imposition of authority by sanctions and brute
force could never be appropriate within a Christian context, if,
indeed, it is in any context. Authority implies a web of relationships
within which a continuing dialogue should exist. Within that web
certain individuals must take responsibility, but any authority that
they exercise must respect all with whom they engage. It is another
manifestation, then, of that same principle which applies to 'rights'
and 'duties'. No one can be guaranteed a right without others seeing

it as their duty to uphold that right. Rights imply duties, as authority implies reasoned acceptance.

Second, and closely related to this principle, authority is exercised most effectively where there is a growth of consensus about how the tradition should be interpreted. This grows out of an understanding of authority rooted in dialogue and reasoned acceptance. It relates to the process of focusing authority within the episcopate, and that itself must also take account of the significance of the lay voice in Anglican patterns of authority. Ecclesiological models will define how the local Churches (the provinces) relate to the communion as a whole. This is one of the crucial issues in developing an *organic* structure of authority within Anglicanism. There is at present lacking an effective symbiosis between the provinces and the communion. Our earlier ecclesiological reflections made it plain that the universal Church can only exist in as much as it is an interdependent network of local Churches. Similarly, if the universal is ignored then the result will be fragmentation and a form of ecclesiological 'tribalism'.

The existence of organic structures of authority, however, itself has certain definitive implications. Organic suggests organism and that implies a living and developing Church. The significance of development has surfaced on a number of occasions throughout this book. Burke's notion of institutions that are open to reform is part of this equation. Since the work of John Henry Newman it has been generally accepted that in some sense (and there is not total unanimity within Christian theology about precisely which sense) Christian doctrine develops. The history of the Christian Church indicates that this is equally true of the institution. This makes any static pattern of authority impossible as a model. The structures of authority themselves need to have built into them an openness to future development, but also checks and balances that help to determine when developments are 'rogue' or fall completely outside the theological, spiritual and moral parameters of the Christian tradition. Anglicanism has embraced this truth by opting for an inductive rather than a deductive approach to development.

Anglicanism and the inductive method

It is now a commonplace that the 'scientific method' is identified with the 'inductive method'. This is obviously not the place to divert into an extended discussion of the philosophy of science, though a brief reflection on the analogy for theology may, however, be useful. In the past five decades a number of different theories have been postulated for the development of scientific hypotheses. These have included theories of verification, falsification and of scientific revolutions.

Each of these changes in fashion, however, has left intact the basic shift which characterises modern science in contrast to the science of the Ancient Greeks. Greek science was rooted in a deductive process founded on a set of *a priori* assumptions about the nature of matter and of the cosmos. Each succeeding principle was thus derived deductively by reflecting upon those basic principles. The shift in modern science, then, was from *a priori* assumptions to a reliance upon observation and practical experimentation. Careful observation and experiment allows the scientist to postulate a theory on the basis of the observed phenomena. This is the essence of the inductive method, and it is still assumed to be the starting-point for the various philosophical theories of science which have followed.

The inductive method, then, is empirical. It is rooted in experience and observation, and in reflection upon that experience and the phenomena observed. By way of analogy, this is the manner in which theology and patterns of authority within Anglicanism have developed. We have already reflected upon the historical roots of the Church of England. It would be oversimplistic to argue that theological issues were insignificant during the long and complex process of Reformation in sixteenth-century England, for throughout this period theology and politics were subtly intertwined. But it would be equally naïve to suggest that there emerged in pristine state at the Elizabethan settlement in 1559 a systematic theology of Anglicanism, or, more accurately, of the Church of England.

The beginnings of a theological apologetic for the Church of

England emerged from the writings of Richard Hooker in his *Laws of Ecclesiastical Polity*. Hooker began, as it were, with what was there before his eyes, the Church of England by law established. Royal supremacy, the Thirty-Nine Articles and the Book of Common Prayer were observable facts upon which the theologian would reflect. Of course, Hooker did not approach his task without any theological presuppositions. The influence of Thomas Aquinas and natural law, for example, are there clearly within his work. In that sense there are also deductive principles involved. The method, however, is clearly one which begins with the facts of history and then attempts to produce both a theological apologetic and principles for an ecclesiology – in Hooker's own words, *Laws of Ecclesiastical Polity*.

Hooker was not alone in tackling the questions in this way. It was a method which was developed by the Caroline moral theologians of the seventeenth century, including Jeremy Taylor, Robert Sanderson and John Sharp.[1] Again, alongside the empirical, historical continuity and the influence of Reformation thought is discernible in the writings of Taylor and others. Nevertheless, the writings of the Caroline divines were characterised by a distinctive Anglican approach to moral theology which was effectively a development of the Western Christian tradition. Here, then, is another area in which the notion of the inductive method and development impinge upon patterns of authority.

This inductive approach is one which has remained characteristic of Anglicanism as it has developed into a world communion. On the local level, patterns of ministry have often developed pragmatically and practically, with a theological underpinning of those patterns following rather than preceding the developments, as would be the case with a deductive approach. Non-stipendiary ministry and the renewal of the diaconate are just two examples; practice preceded theology. One can also argue that instruments of communion have developed similarly. We are still in the process of extrapolating a clear theology of authority, but this in itself is not a new experience for Anglicans. The establishment of the Lambeth Conference, for example, preceded the writing of the Lambeth

Quadrilateral and other later theological documents relating to ecclesiology.

In following this inductive method, the style and approach of Anglicanism contrasts sharply with that of Roman Catholicism which is grounded in a deductive method, rooted very clearly in a dogmatic approach to tradition. In adopting such a method Anglicanism embraces a tradition of pragmatism, where often the pastoral and the contingent are built into the structures of authority. One might argue that here Anglicanism is resonant with the empirical traditions frequently encountered in those places where 'Anglo-Saxon' patterns of thought have dominated. Roman Catholicism is more strongly influenced by patterns of Roman law. Within Roman Catholicism, pastoral considerations still often apply in matters relating to authoritative teaching, but the application is adjusted by the way in which the law itself is administered. The contrast, then, is with Anglican patterns of dispersed authority. There are good reasons for defending this inductive approach. It builds into patterns of authority an organic means for allowing both institutions and their teaching to develop. The contingent is taken seriously, but in clear conjunction with the tradition. The result is an appropriately developmental sense of authority.

From autonomy to interdependence

It is in relation to the much-prized autonomy of independent provinces that Anglican patterns of dispersed authority are most frequently criticised. This autonomy relates strongly to the history of the communion. The republicanism which influenced the development of the Episcopal Church of the United States of America has been seminal. The establishment of overseas bishoprics elsewhere often laid similar foundations. The transformation of the British Empire into a Commonwealth of autonomous independent nation states has reinforced this cherishing of autonomy within the provinces in more recent decades. But what precisely is being claimed in the defence of autonomy?

The *Shorter Oxford English Dictionary* defines autonomy as 'the right of self-government' or, on the individual level, 'personal freedom'. One of the dangers is that these two rather different definitions are allowed to elide into each other. Self-government, which seems a perfectly proper and healthy property to cherish, becomes exaggerated to embrace a freedom which fails to take seriously our dependence upon each other and our need to respect each other. It is the same problem that we encountered when talking of duties and rights, but starting from the other end of the equation. This time it is an insufficient appreciation of the duties we owe to others. Seen from one direction, authority is a problem because it does not issue from dialogue; it is imposed. Seen from the other direction, authority is a problem because an individual or group does not recognise her/his/its duties to others. Freedom is seen as absolute and ultimately collapses into solipsism.

A healthy view of autonomy, that recognises appropriate self-government and the maturity of different communities and cultures across the world, was well rehearsed by Bishop Stephen Bayne, one-time executive officer of the Anglican Communion. At the 1963 Anglican Congress in Toronto, Bayne argued:

> The Anglican communion is not an organisation by which older and stronger Churches can extend their influence over younger and weaker Churches. We are not interested in branch offices around the world. We care rather for a household within which many Churches, representing many cultures and peoples, can take their self-reliant and buoyant place in full brother-hood, each giving and teaching, each receiving and learning. Therefore our organisation must both reflect this and nourish it.[2]

The instinct in Stephen Bayne's description is balanced and healthy, but even so there is at least one point of danger. Bayne refers to Churches as being self-reliant. There is a difficulty here in placing self-reliance alongside the New Testament witness. The image of the crucified Christ is one of self-giving rather than self-reliance. Responsibility for oneself, of course, does not stand contrary to the Christian tradition, but a bald assertion of self-reliance does. Bayne is rightly concerned that Churches (provinces) should respect each other and not impose their will upon each other. In the context of the early 1960s it may be that this point is political; the Americans were understandably keen to emphasise the integrity of each province, and the perils of an unhealthy dependence upon the see of Canterbury. This principle, however, is still in danger of being applied *ad absurdum*.

In such circumstances, separate provinces are unlikely to give and teach, to receive and learn. This is one aspect of a particular sort of contemporary Western individualism that is easily applied to institutions as well as to people. Such an attitude easily ignores how much each individual is dependent upon others for her/his character and flourishing. It is self-evidently true of children in relation to parents, but it is equally true of our dependence upon each other within the wider webs of society. One of the reasons for general abhorrence of suicide is that one person's death not only extinguishes that single human life, but in doing so it diminishes all who are around him. Ought not all the provinces to agree that, on certain classes of doctrinal matters, they should voluntarily bind themselves to consult the primates, and if necessary other 'instruments of communion', before making changes? That should be a minimum mutual obligation.

Extreme caricatures of autonomy and independence, then, are vulnerable to the same criticisms of extreme forms of subjectivism and relativism. An individual or a community becomes isolated from all other neighbours. The process of learning, teaching, giving and receiving which Bayne describes becomes impossible. Furthermore, any sense of communion will eventually atrophy. On such a model, Anglicanism would soon fragment into a series of independent and unrelated gathered Churches in different parts of the world. There would remain little or no global perspective. Archbishop Runcie responded to such exaggerated patterns of autonomy and independence at the 1988 Lambeth Conference:

> [O]ur own global experience as a world communion also teaches us the importance of a global perspective at a time

when political concerns for 'national security' often militate against international co-operation and diminish the significance of world organisations such as the United Nations.

Developing this argument, the archbishop reflected directly on the subject which we are exploring. As he reviewed the notion of the absolute independence of provinces, he noted:

> The New Testament speaks more in terms of *interdependence* than *independence*. The relationship of Jesus with the Father in the bond of the Holy Spirit as witnessed in St John's Gospel surely gives us the pattern of Christian relationship. Life together in communion implies basic trust and mutuality. . . . The good of the Body requires mutual recognition and deference in Christ.[3]

In arguing for deference and for interdependence, one is not denying the need for self-government nor the need to respect our sisters and brothers individually, or institutionally within local Churches. John Zizioulas argues: 'All structures aiming at facilitating the universality of the Church create a *network of Communion of Churches, not a new form of Church*.'[4]

Zizioulas's description captures the subtlety of the relationship between the local and the universal. The danger is always one of oversimplification. Either the individual and local are seen as primary with little note taken of the universal, or vice versa. It is a similar problem to that which Christians have experienced with regard to Trinitarian theology. There is a continual tendency either to emphasise unity at the expense of diversity or diversity at the expense of unity.

Within Anglicanism it is crucial for provinces to develop sufficient trust in each other so that mutual respect engenders a real feeling of interdependence. The focal position of the archbishop of Canterbury can assist in this by building a model where all honour the primacy of Canterbury as the centre of an interdependent network of Churches. The Chair of Augustine acts as a focus. This should help avoid tension between provinces caused by fear of threat and interference. It offers the opportunity of developing a healthy web of interrelated and interdependent Churches, but for this to be effective the role of the archbishop of Canterbury must not, however, become exaggerated. If expectations upon the archbishop, his leadership and his authority grow out of proportion, other difficulties will arise. A different form of unhealthy dependence may emerge, and in other quarters this will generate threat and suspicion that an Anglican papal model is evolving. All this requires a delicate balance. The relationship between the archbishop and the Primates' Meeting is one of the essential ingredients, as indeed is the relationship between the Primates' Meeting and the synodical structures of individual provinces.

At present the Inter-Anglican Doctrinal Commission is giving its corporate mind to the issues of 'communion' and 'instruments of communion'. It is doing so in response to Resolution 18 of the 1988 Lambeth Conference which noted that there should be: 'As a matter of urgency further exploration of the meaning and nature of communion with particular reference to the doctrine of the trinity, the unity and order of the Church, and the unity and community of humanity.'

An initial report, *Belonging Together*, was published in 1992 by the commission, and this latest document is a response to the 1992 report. Drafts of this later report indicate that it will ask a series of questions to the various instruments of authority within the communion. It holds back, however, from making specific recommendations, although it does in a second appendix put forward for discussion the possibility of establishing a regular series of 'Anglican Congresses'. Later in this chapter, and independently of the commission's deliberations, the establishment of a regular Anglican Congress is mooted. The difference in the proposals here centre on its place within the international authority structures of Anglicanism. Might it be possible for such a regular congress to assume the place at present occupied by the Anglican Consultative Council? If it did so, then there ought to be close integration of such a congress into the other Anglican instruments of communion; it would not be solely consultative, as in the case of the present Anglican Consultative Council.

Primates *inter pares?*

Some of the issues which are crucial to appropriate models of leadership and authority in the Anglican Communion bear equally upon the role of the archbishop of Canterbury within the Church of England. Recent discussion of models of authority there illuminate similar issues on the level of the Anglican Communion. Hugh Dickinson wrote of the role of the archbishop of Canterbury within the Church of England:

> From the Chair of St Augustine the Primate can bend the hearts of the whole community towards the healing of national wounds and the feeding of the nation's spiritual hunger. The Chair of St Augustine is not the seat of the Chairman of the C. of E. PLC.[5]

As our earlier chapters have demonstrated, this is equally true of the archbishop of Canterbury's role within the communion. It is not sufficient, however, simply to accept the *status quo* in terms of the respect and honour with which the Chair of St Augustine is held. There needs to be a clarity within the structures which defines and supports this role and holds it in balance in relation to other instruments of communion. Dickinson makes this point in relation to the Church of England. If the House of Bishops is not adequately serviced and if insufficient time is given to consultation, then the archbishop's role will equally fall out of balance. The same is true of the Anglican Communion. The Primates' Meeting is compact enough to offer to the communion the sense of focus, interdependence and regular consultation that is necessary to sustain and nurture communion. The picture painted earlier of the 1995 Primates' Meeting in Windsor saw the archbishop of Canterbury focusing the work of all the primates, but in a manner that allows each to contribute from his own expertise and cultural experience. The richness, diversity and unity of the communion can be facilitated by such a model. It is a small enough body for personal links and loyalties to be forged; this in itself is an essential ingredient. Nevertheless, there is still far too little clarity about the interdependence of different structures and even the *raison d'être* of some of the present bodies.

The answer may lie in a better serviced Primates' Meeting (at present the Anglican Communion Office staff is overstretched and expected to be omnicompetent in supporting all the inter-Anglican bodies), where an officer is seconded for five or six years from one province to service the primates. Such secondments would defuse fears of a burgeoning inter-Anglican bureaucracy. The primates should meet regularly so that rapport is built up on a personal level. There should be a clear integration of the Primates' Meeting with provincial synods. Where there is a specific issue for debate – be it polygamy, liturgical consensus or the support of missionary dioceses – one provincial synod, with the leadership of its House of Bishops, might be commissioned to report upon and debate the issue and then refer it back to the Primates' Meeting. This would retain the role of 'bishops in synod' and also the key Anglican principle of the lay voice within the councils of the Church. There might also be an argument for gathering together the lay chairs/presidents of provincial synods – again, this would be a compact body, and it would need to be given a clear authority in *certain areas* and a structured relationship with the Primates' Meeting.

The role of the Anglican Consultative Council is at present uncertain. It is an expensive body to convene, simply in terms of numbers. It has no legislative power, and its relationship to both the Primates' Meeting and the individual provincial synod is unclear. It may be most courageous for the communion to think again about this. The council is itself a child of the Lambeth Conference which, alongside the office of the archbishop of Canterbury, must be considered to be one of the two *primary* instruments of communion. There ought to be the freedom to construct and then reconstruct effective bodies for the maintenance of communion and for the appropriate exercising of authority. This should be true within all Churches, confessions and communions. The establishment of the

Anglican Consultative Council was an attempt to incorporate within the international instruments of communion a body which incarnated the Anglican principle of the lay voice within the government of the Church. The principle is right, but the present model cumbersome and ineffective. Without any real authority such a body simply pays lip-service to the principle of lay involvement.

Ought there instead to be a reversion to periodic international Anglican congresses, perhaps timed to coincide with Lambeth Conferences? It may then be essential to limit the bishops attending Lambeth Conferences to diocesans. Where there is an imbalance in numbers from provinces, it may be that not even all diocesans from one province should come but an elected proportion. Alongside the Lambeth Conference, and for part of the time combined with it, would go a compact congress bringing together lay people and priests from throughout the provinces. This would produce a more *organic* model and the structures would be deliberately interrelated.

None of these patterns would eliminate the essential leadership roles of either the archbishop of Canterbury throughout the communion, or of individual primates within their own provinces. Primates would seek to focus consensus within their own province, but they would also perform the crucial function traditionally expected of the episcopate, that is, they would communicate the consensus of their own province and provincial synod to the worldwide councils of Anglicanism, and at the same time pass on to their provinces the concerns of the communion. This is the intention at present, but the structures are not sufficiently clear and the servicing and support networks are inadequate to allow this to happen really effectively. Given clearer structures, each primate will effectively offer a higher profile for his province. It will be a case of 'primates *inter pares*', with the Chair of Augustine as the universal focus still within the communion.

Benedictine resonances

Early on in this book, the patterns established by Benedict in his Rule were extolled. They are patterns that have proved themselves within community for the past 1500 years. They are patterns, however, that, under closer scrutiny, may be less fashionable in an age that places patterns of parliamentary democracy near the top of the political pantheon. Even the Church in its synodical structures has attempted to embrace patterns that are sometimes pale imitations of the political models in the country from which they originate. Not all Anglican synodical structures are identical, but generally they all pay lip-service to political models of democracy. Is this really appropriate, particularly at a time when even Western patterns of democracy have been at least partially discredited?

The starting-point in answer to that question is not an attack on the principles or even the mechanics of democracy. Rather, it is to say that the authority structures within the Christian Church do not parallel those of nation states. Authority is related to a community of belief. Authority structures need to be capable of expressing that belief and discerning appropriate developments. In this context, the patterns established by Benedict of the 'abbot in chapter' are more appropriate to the Church, since the aim must be to focus consensus within the community. It is interesting to note that often cathedral and other monastic chapter houses are circular or octagonal in shape. The design reflects the model of a community meeting together to discern what the community as a whole believes. Authority issues from the consensus of the community.

This model is one which is equally important within Roman Catholicism when the Church talks of the *sensus fidelium*. At the heart of any understanding of the *sensus fidelium* is the issue of the value to be accorded to the insights of the faithful in relation to the statements of the Church on matters of authority. In other words, the precise part that the lay voice has to play is also a matter of issue in the Roman Catholic Church and not only in Anglicanism. Jean-Marie Tillard writes:

> The *sensus fidelium* implies infinitely more, at least in the eyes of Roman Catholic tradition, than just a force of balance or positive criticism towards hierarchical decisions. . . . It is also the bearer of a conviction on which the *magisterium* itself must

draw when it feels the need to affirm the content of the faith in the most authoritative manner at its disposal.[6]

Roman Catholic theologians have thus argued that both the statement of Vatican I declaring the infallibility of the papacy, and the 1951 Declaration on Marian Dogma articulated authoritative teaching which truly represented the *sensus fidelium*. Such beliefs, it is contended, were already there within the hearts of the faithful well before the declarations were made officially. But such an argument has, of course, equal force when substantial numbers of lay people argue for innovation. There are increasing numbers of Roman Catholics arguing that the priesthood should be open to women. It would be a gross exaggeration to suggest that this is, at present, a majority Roman Catholic view worldwide. The question can be put, however, as to how the hierarchy would respond if and when this did become the accepted consensus within the Church, particularly in the light of a papal declaration which argues that the Church does not have the authority to innovate in such matters.

Behind such debates also stand issues of 'reception' within the Church. How does the Anglican Communion decide when the principle of ordaining women to the priesthood has been 'received' by the Church worldwide? Presumably, one possible criterion by which to judge might be when all provincial synods have expressed their acceptance of such a principle. Officially, that must be the means of discerning an authoritative decision, although within the Episcopal Church in the USA and in the Church of England there are still substantial minorities who have not yet been able to receive such doctrines. This is in itself an indicator that the principle of democratic debate is not a final means of arriving at consensus, nor, indeed, of arriving at authoritative decisions.

It would be oversimplistic to apply the Benedictine pattern direct to synods and councils, but there are principles that can inform the process. In an article which looked primarily at the growth of individuals within community, the sometime abbot-primate of the Benedictines, Dom Rembert Weakland, offered insights which are equally applicable to communities as a whole and to groups within communities. He write, for example, at one point:

> It is by means of the guidance of the Gospel that one arrives at that necessary love and faith. I would repeat, therefore, that the role of authority is simply to keep the Gospel constantly before the monks, before the mind of every member of the community, before the community as community, and before the monks as individuals.[7]

This is, of course, not so very different from the teaching role of the bishops within the councils of the Church. Authority is not imposed, but it arises out of dialogue and reflection within the community. A little later on, Weakland addressed directly the issue of diversity in unity. He wrote:

> Maybe in our day especially, when so many people are critical of their bishops, we have something to learn from this. We have to see beyond the personal weaknesses of superiors and see the need we have for a centre of unity. The more pluralism we have in the Benedictine Confederation, the more need for an Abbot-Primate, pardon my saying so; and the more pluralism one admits into a community, the more need for an abbot as a point of unity.[8]

These reflections upon pluralism and diversity speak directly to the subject in hand. The role of the abbot in chapter, furthermore, parallels at least to some degree the role of bishops in synod. In clarifying structures at the heart of Anglicanism it is these issues that stand paramount. Are there areas of competence and responsibility, particularly in doctrine and liturgy, that should be under the guardianship of the bishops? If this is so, how should the *sensus fidelium* be gauged if it is not to be achieved through the democracy of crude majority voting? A close co-operation between provincial houses of bishops/synods and the Primates' Meeting is one step. More regular meetings of the primates, fed by input from the provinces, is a second step. Anglican congresses held in a symbiotic relationship with Lambeth Conferences is a third element. A clearer sense of the archbishop of Canterbury as the focus of, but not overdominant in, the Primates' Meeting might be the final element. All of these elements require the establishment of a clear but organic set of structures. It requires courage, too, in reforming and even abolishing present structures where they are inadequate or inappropriate to their tasks.

There is often a temptation to view history through rose-tinted spectacles. The grass was always greener in earlier centuries. The introduction to this book gives the lie to such romantic notions. Augustine's role was tough and pioneering; he did not always find his mission easy or even attractive. The Church in the seventh century was not monochrome nor, indeed, agreed in all its parts. The celebrated debate over the dating of Easter is but one example of diversity that was not easily reconciled. Ultimately, however, despite interventions from politicians and often bitter disagreement, a network of parishes sprang up which covered the whole of Europe. Augustine was the pioneering primate of just one fragmentary part of that continent and of that early Church. The pattern of which Augustine's Church was one part has been replicated not only in Europe but more recently has covered the world. The dazzling array of different contemporary cultures has made the task of preserving a true unity in diversity, locality with universality, even more difficult to achieve. Nevertheless, Anglicanism has, within its multi-varied roots and its historic continuity, both within Western Catholicism and within the Reformation tradition, the potential to contribute much to the universal Church of God in patterns of leadership and authority. It can only begin to do this by asking radical questions first of itself.

Notes

Chapter 1

1 Simon Schama, *Citizens*, Penguin, London, 1989, p.3.
2 See Conor Cruise O'Brien, *The Great Melody*, Sinclair Stevenson, London, 1992, and Edmund Burke, *Reflections upon the Revolution in France*, Penguin Electra, Harmondsworth, 1986.
3 See particularly J.H. Plumb, *The Death of the Past*, Penguin, Harmondsworth, 1973.
4 See G.R. Dunstan, *The Artifice of Ethics*, SCM Press, London, 1974.
5 Plumb, op cit., p.17.
6 Ibid, p.44.
7 Peter Berger, *A Rumour of Angels*, Allen Lane, The Penguin Press, London, 1970.
8 Ibid, p.70.
9 Ibid., loc. cit.
10 Ibid., p.73.
11 Joseph Fletcher, *Situation Ethics*, SCM Press, London, 1966, which immortalised the term for the Christian Churches.
12 J.L. Mackie, *Ethics – Inventing Right and Wrong*, Penguin, Harmondsworth, 1977.
13 Basil Mitchell, *Faith and Criticism*, Clarendon Press, Oxford, 1994, especially Chapter 8.
14 See, for example, the works of Lesslie Newbigin, *Foolishness to the Greeks* (London, SPCK, 1986), *The Other Side of 1984* (Geneva, WCC, 1983) and Hugh Montefiore (ed.), *The Gospel and Contemporary Culture* (Mowbray, London, 1992).
15 This point is cogently made by James Barr in his *Fundamentalism*, SCM Press, London, 1977.
16 See, for example, the work of Maurice Wiles and particularly *The Remaking of Christian Doctrine*, SCM Press, London, 1974.

17 Plumb, op. cit., p.37.

18 Ibid., pp.90–1

19 Robert Runcie, *Authority in Crisis?*, SCM Press, London, 1988, p.8.

20 Op. cit., p.10.

21 In recent years, further transformations in thought, related to the Enlightenment but pressing forward its implications still more sharply, have taken place. Following the Second World War different strands of thought, but with certain elements in common, gained the name 'post-modernism'. Theological discourse has not been immune to the effects of such currents of thought: see Don Cupitt, *Taking Leave of God* (SCM Press, London 1980) and more recently Anthony Freeman, *God In Us* (SCM Press, London, 1993). An Anglican parish priest, Freeman was deprived of his licence by authority of his bishop because of the nature of his writings.

22 The response to *Humanae Vitae* in developed Western countries shows clearly the challenge to be faced; many of the faithful have made their own decision in the teeth of official authority.

Chapter 2

1 See Dennis Nineham, *The Gospel According to St Mark*, Penguin, Harmondsworth, 1963, pp.106, 108.

2 Quoted in R. Sencourt, *T.S. Eliot*, Garnstone Press, 1971, p.116.

3 Eamon Duffy, *The Stripping of the Altars*, Yale University Press, New Haven, Conn., 1992.

4 Christopher Haigh, *English Reformations*, Clarendon Press, Oxford, 1993.

5 Ibid., p.95.

6 G.R. Elton, *The Tudor Constitution*, CUP, Cambridge, 1965, p.368.

7 Cited in A. Richardson, *Preface to Bible Study*, Philadelphia, Westminster, 1944.

8 Richard Hooker, *Laws of Ecclesiastical Polity*, Book I, Preface, Chapter 3.

9 Don Cupitt, *Taking Leave of God*, p.166. Probably the most famous and infamous exponent of such an approach is the Cambridge theologian, Don Cupitt. At the end of his first book which expounded non-realist Christianity, he wrote: 'I continue to speak of God, to pray to God. God is the mythical embodiment of all that one is concerned with in the spiritual life. He is the religious demand and ideal, the pearl of great price, and the enshriner of values. He is needed – but as a myth.'

10 Roger Coleman (ed.), *Resolutions of the Twelve Lambeth Conferences, 1867–1988*, Anglican Book Centre, Toronto, 1992, p.13.

11 Hooker, op. cit., Book VIII, Chapter 6.10.

12 See Fergus Kerr's reflections in *New Blackfriars*, 1979, April (vol. 60, no. 707) to November (vol. 60, no. 713) and January (vol. 61, no. 716).

13 Dom Paul Grammont OSB, and Dom Philibert Zoebel OSB, 'The

Authority of the Indwelling World', in John M. Todd (ed.), *Problems of Authority*, London, 1962.

14 David Parry OSB, *Households of God*, Darton, Longman and Todd, London, 1980, p.36.

Chapter 3

1 Clifford Longley, 'The Crisis-strewn Roads to Freedom', *The Times*, 2 March 1987.
2 Ibid.
3 For a detailed account, see Richard Southern, *St Anselm: Portrait in a Landscape*, CUP, Cambridge, 1990, especially Chapters 12 and 14.
4 See David Newsome, *The Convert Cardinals*, John Murray, London, 1993, pp.62ff.
5 Ibid., quoted by Newsome, p.63.
6 Quoted in Adrian Hastings, *A History of English Christianity, 1920–1985*, Collins, London, 1986, p.207.
7 *Working As One Body*, Church House Publishing, London, 1995.
8 Parry, op. cit., p.24.
9 Longley, op. cit.

Chapter 4

1 The Church of Bangladesh (alongside the Churches of North and South India and Pakistan) is a 'united Church'. Formed through the coming together of Anglicans with members of other reformed Churches within an episcopal framework, these Churches are now full members of the Anglican Communion while remaining in communion also with their other founding Churches (variously Methodist, Presbyterian, Congregationalist, Lutheran).
2 See for example, in relation to Africa, Adrian Hastings, *Robert Runcie*, Mowbray, London, 1991, p.148.
3 William Jacob, *The Making of the Anglican Communion*, SPCK, London (to be published 1997). See his conclusion. I am greatly indebted to Bill Jacob for the historical background in this chapter.
4 Roger Coleman (ed.), *Resolutions of the Twelve Lambeth Conferences, 1867–1988*, Anglican Book Centre, Toronto, 1992, p.1.
5 John Howe, *Anglicanism and the Universal Church*, Anglican Book Centre, Toronto, 1990, p.63.
6 Alan M.G. Stephenson, *Anglicanism and the Lambeth Conferences*, SPCK, London, 1978, p.48.
7 Jacob, op.cit., ch. 7.
8 *Minutes of Joint Meeting of Primates and the Standing Committee of the*

Anglican Consultative Council, Larnaca, Cyprus, 2 May 1989. Appendix A, The Anglican Communion: Identity and Authority.

Chapter 5

1 Vera Rich, *The Tablet*, 9 March 1996, p.342.
2 Serge Keleher, 'Who's Who in the Divided Orthodox World?', *The Tablet*, 9 March 1996, p.345.
3 See H. Mayr-Harting, *The Coming of Christianity to Anglo-Saxon England*, London, 1972, 1991.
4 See Richard McBrien, *Catholicism*, 3rd edition, Mowbray, London, 1994, p.597.
5 See John Zizioulas, *Being as Communion*, St Vladimir's Seminary Press, New York, 1985, p.148.
6 Ibid., p.149.
7 Ibid., p.258.
8 Disagreements over the precise role of the ecumenical patriarch are well explored by Elie Mélia in his essay, 'An Orthodox Point of View on the Problem of Authority in the Church', in John M. Todd (ed.), *Problems of Authority*, Darton, Longman and Todd, London, 1962, pp.104 ff.
9 J.-M. Tillard, *Eglise des Eglises* (translated as *Church of Churches: The Ecclesiology of Communion*, Liturgical Press, Collegeville, Minn., 1992).
10 *Lumen Gentium* 26, in Austin Flannery OP (ed.), *Vatican II*, English Edition, New York, 1975, p.381.
11 Ibid., and here quoting the Byzantine rite.
12 Ibid., p.382.
13 *Church as Communion*, Anglican–Roman Catholic International Commission II, Church House Publishing/Catholic Truth Society, London, 1991, para. 24.

Chapter 6

1 Adrian Hastings, 'SOS Bosnia', *Theology*, vol. XCVII, no. 778, July/August 1994, pp.242 ff.
2 *Together in Mission and Ministry*, The Porvöo Common Statement, Church House Publishing, London, 1993, p.8, para.8.
3 Ibid., p.22, para.34.
4 Ibid., ch. IV.
5 Stephen Sykes, *The Integrity of Anglicanism*, Mowbray, London, 1978.
6 Thomas Hardy, *Far from the Madding Crowd*, ch. 42.
7 Sykes, op. cit., p.85.
8 Ibid., p.93. See also, 'Introduction: Why Authority', in Stephen Sykes (ed.), *Authority in the Anglican Communion*, Toronto, 1987, p.19. Here he notes:

Notes

'There are already clear signs that an instructed and active Roman Catholic laity are unlikely to be satisfied with the role of passivity inside the structures of the church assigned them by the unmodified retention of hierarchical government.'

9 Ibid., p.99.

10 Sara Maitland, *A Big-Enough God: Artful Theology*, Mowbray, London, 1995, pp.8–9.

11 Ibid., p.99.

12 William A. Norgren and William G. Rusch (eds), *Toward Full Communion* and *Concordat of Agreement*, Lutheran–Episcopal Dialogue, Series III, Augsburg Press, Minneapolis, and Forward Movement Publications, Cincinnati, 1991.

Chapter 7

1 Evelyn Waugh, *Decline and Fall*, Penguin, Harmondsworth, 1928, p.33.

2 This theme has been developed separately in the paper *Apostolicity and Succession*, General Synod, General Synod Publication (House of Bishops' Occasional Paper), London, 1994. Emphasis on the validity of the orders of individuals can easily take one down the road followed by *episcopi vagantes*.

3 Porvöo, op. cit., p.31.

4 *Report of the Archbishop of Canterbury's Commission on Communion and Women in the Episcopate*, Final Verson, Anglican Book Centre, Toronto, 1994.

5 Robert Runcie, *The Unity We Seek*, SCM Press, London, 1989, p.9.

7 *Declaration on the Admission of Women to the Ministerial Priesthood* (*Inter Insignores*), 1976.

8 Runcie, op. cit., p.16.

9 John Goldingay, 'Charismatic Spirituality: Some Theological Reflections', *Theology*, May/June 1996, vol. XCIX, no. 789, p.186.

10 Runcie, op. cit., p.7.

11 *One in Hope*, CHP/CTS, London, 1989, pp.13, 14.

12 Ibid., p.21.

Chapter 8

1 David Lodge, *The British Museum is Falling Down*, Penguin, Harmondsworth, 1983, pp.8, 11–12.

2 *Life in Christ: Morals, Communion and the Church*, Church House Publishing/Catholic Truth Society, London, 1994, p.19.

3 Albert Schweitzer, *The Quest of the Historical Jesus*, English translation, 1910, p.397.

4 R.H. Lightfoot, *History and Interpretation in the Gospels*, Hodder and Stoughton, London, 1935, p.225.

5 D.E. Nineham *The Use and Abuse of the Bible*, Macmillan, London, 1976.

6 For an even-handed critique and appreciation of Nineham's arguments, see John Barton, Reflections on Cultural Relativism, I & II, *Theology*, March/May 1979, vol. LXXXII, no. 686, pp.103–9, and vol. LXXXII, no. 687, pp.191–9.

7 *Homosexual Relationships: A Contribution to Discussion*, CIO Publishing, London, 1979, p.33.

8 *Peake's Commentary on the Bible*, A. & C. Black, London, 1962: 'The Authority of the Bible', pp.1–7.

9 Coleman, op. cit., p.121.

10 Ibid., p.122, Resolutions 9–12.

11 *ARCIC I Final Report*, SPCK/Catholic Truth Society, London, 1982, p.52, para. 2.

12 Ibid., pp.69–71.

13 J.L. Houlden (ed.), *The Interpretation of the Bible in the Church*, SCM Press, London, 1995, p.82.

14 *Issues in Human Sexuality: A Statement by the House of Bishops*, Church House, London, 1991, p.1.

15 Ibid., p.41.

Chapter 9

1 Robert Runcie, *Windows on to God*, SPCK, London, 1983, p.1.

2 Ibid., pp.3–4.

3 Paul Vallely, 'Simple preacher tries on a pontiff's robes', *The Independent*, 29 May 1996.

4 Encyclical Letter, *Ut Unum Sint*, of the Holy Father John Paul II on Commitment to Ecumenism, Rome, 25 May 1995.

5 Vallely, op. cit.

6 See *Working as One Body*, Church House Publishing, London, 1995, and subsequent synod papers and reports of debates.

Chapter 10

1 Runcie, *Windows on to God*, p.5.

2 H. Richard Niebuhr, *Christ and Culture*, Harper and Row, New York, 1951.

3 Ibid., p.231.

4 Giles Ecclestone, *The Church of England and Politics*, CIO Publishing, London, 1981, p.61.

5 Ibid., p.65.

6 George Carey, *Sharing a Vision*, Darton, Longman and Todd, London, 1993, p.97.

7 Hansard, 5 July 1996, HMSO, London, p.1693.

8 Coleman (ed.), *Resolutions of the Lambeth Conferences*, p.218.

9 Ibid., p.229.

10 Niebuhr, op. cit., p.196.

11 Colin Craston, 'Continuing the Story 1984–1990', in Howe, *Anglicanism and the Universal Church*.

12 Coleman, op. cit., p.44.

Chapter 11

1 See H.R. McAdoo's excellent analysis in *The Structure of Caroline Moral Theology*, Longmans, Green, London, 1949.

2 Howe, op. cit., p.79.

3 Hastings, *Runcie*, p.153.

4 Zizioulas, op. cit., p.258.

5 Hugh Dickinson, 'What Our Bishops Lack', *Church Times*, 9 February 1996.

6 J.M.R. Tillard, quoted in Gillian Evans, *Method in Ecumenical Theology*, CUP, Cambridge, 1996, p.198.

7 Rembert Weakland, 'Growth through Authority', *Tjurunga*, 14, 1977, p.80.

8 Ibid., p.89.

Index

Index

Index

Index

Index